To: The youngsters who died in the New Cross Fire, 1981, Antony Birkbeck, Humphrey Brown, Peter Campbell, Patrick Cummings, Steve Collins, Jerry Francis, Andrew Gooding, Lloyd Hall, Lillian Henry, Patricia Johnson, Glen Powell, Owen Thompson, Yvonne Ruddock and Paul Ruddock.

From: eachoneteachone.org.uk 20th January 2001.

1991, Rolan Adams, 1992, Rohit Duggal and Stephen Lawrence 1993, Antony Walker, Michael Brown and Ahmed Iqbal Ullah.

ACKNOWLEDGEMENTS

Thanks to Myra Berg, Ansel Wong, Carey Robinson and Hansib Publications for their comments and support.

An African Journey

BOOK TWO

From Emancipation 1838 to 1948
The Windrush and the 'Mother Country'

Barbara E. Ellis

First published in Great Britain by Hansib Publications in 2018

Hansib Publications Limited
P.O. Box 226, Hertford SG14 3WY UK

info@hansibpublications.com
www.hansibpublications.com

ISBN 978-1-910553-91-6

A CIP catalogue record for this book
is available from the British Library

Production by Hansib Publications Limited

CONTENTS

INTRODUCTION

In their working, sleeping and waking hours the fixation of the enslaved people was to free themselves from the cane pieces of the Americas. Liberation would enhance their earnings in the flourishing Sunday markets, more land and a realistic wage would achieve their post-emancipation financial, political and social goals. They would exploit and capitalise on their hard-earned freedom, as they were now in control of their future and destiny they reasoned.

If the enslaved Africans' pursuit of liberation had been protracted and harrowing, their goals for economic and political autonomy would be even harder to achieve after 1838. Political and financial independence should have logically followed from their emancipation. However, the plantocracy and their government intervened to maintain their economic power and control. Their policies and practices guaranteed that the economic and political objectives of the Africans would be elusive and almost impossible to achieve. The bountiful and generous islands and mainland that had enriched them and their governments would not provide the monetary autonomy, the free Africans had fought for and were entitled to.

The liberated people would have to wander near and far to get the most basic remuneration for their labour. Their yearning to improve their and their kinfolk's basic needs would be blocked at every stage by the colonial administration. They would keep them as close to economic enslavement as was legally possible. They were the biblical 'Israelites', as referred to by Desmond Dekker in his 1968 song of the same name; he is a descendant of the enslaved people. Graphically, the singer and songwriter summed up the chronic condition of his ancestors and the generations from liberty through to political independence and beyond. Economic self-determination would be a difficult and almost impossible aspiration to achieve for the masses in the colonised islands and the mainland. Decade after decade they would have to move from continent to continent seeking the most elementary economic rewards for their valuable labour.

Harold Macmillan's 1960, 'winds of change' speech, made on the African continent, blew away the cobwebs of the British Empire. It replaced its exploitative machinery in the colonies with political independence, administered by small Black and Brown ruling elites, flags, parliaments and bureaucracies that maintained and boosted its influence and monetary accumulation. The proxy neo-colonial ruling elite would block and suppress the political, economic aspirations and social advancement of the overzealous freed people, for their former masters.

The colonialists and their surrogates' task was to maintain the exploitative socio-economic system of capitalism and imperialism in the former colonies. This had made the Africans jump at the opportunity to improve their economic status in the mother country as invited workers from 1948, although they were not the first choice of the British bureaucrats to rebuild Britain after the devastation of World War II. They would make up the short fall in labour the Old Commonwealth and Europe could not provide. As the second choice workforce of the mother country, their experiences would mirror the struggles of their ancestors in the cane pieces of the 'Enslaved World'.

Daily, they would face racism and discrimination, they would continually strive to be acknowledged as equal and viable human beings. Continuously, they would have to fight to get decent schooling and housing for themselves and their children as well as economic and social mobility, via the education system. Equality and financial security would elude the children of the Windrush's generation in the mother country.

CHAPTER 1

Whose story?

"I do not want to hear any more 'Anancy stories'," snapped the old and wrinkled aristocrat as he disdainfully confronted his opponents. "I know only too well the story of the British slave trade and slavery. It was my ancestors and a generation of brave and fearless men, who moulded and fashioned the plantation system with their bare hands. Those groundbreakers, many of them with a couple of Irish indentured servants, ripped up the gut-wrenching forests of St Kitts, Barbados, and Nevis. They planted tobacco; a crop that broke their backs and deformed their limbs as they yanked a living from those harsh terrains, with their miserable harvests. A hellish existence best describes the lives of those early trailblazers in St Kitts and Barbados," the old boy stated proudly.

"Fortuitously, for them, our arch rivals the Portuguese colonialists and their Dutch financiers; transferred sugar growing and vast numbers of Negroes from the fringes of their West African coastal plantations to Brazil. Sugar grew profusely on Brazil's virgin soil. Naturally, my ancestors ripped up the tobacco and planted sugar instead. It was at this point that their hard work and sacrifice rewarded them with a crop, that transformed their lives and fortunes immediately. From then on, they worked tirelessly to develop the sugar industry in Barbados, later those diligent pioneers took it and exported it to the colonies in the islands and the Americas, giving the United Kingdom the wealth to develop and sustain its industries and Empire," he smiled.

"Those innovators continued to shape and mould plantation slavery, to maximise their profits and make the plantations self-sufficient within Barbados, until they were forced to give up their profitable business enterprise in 1807 and 1838, by our Government. Consider the wealth created by the ingenuity of those early visionaries, imagine the effect on Africa and its population who benefited greatly from the wealth that was being created. Yes, my ancestors did not pay their slaves, but they clothed, fed and housed them and their families. They also allowed them to grow and sell crops from their small plots and provision grounds, to feed themselves and make a little money, those plantation owners were very generous indeed," he stated self-righteously.

"The European slave traders put money in the pockets of the African traders, and middle men on the coast, who caught and sold their own brothers and sisters to them. Therefore, the continent profited too. The trickle-down effect it is called. Consequently, everyone benefited, especially those Africans who were dying of disease in their thousands before we came and rescued them. It is an indisputable fact, that our slaves lived happier and more rewarding lives, on our estates and plantations in the Americas growing crops; than they would have done in war-torn and diseased Africa. Daily, we gave them productive work, religion, trade and some food. Our contribution to Africa and its people cannot be dismissed or devalued," he spat out.

Self-righteously, he continued.

"We gave Africa and its people Christianity, commerce, and our great civilisation. Yes, in time we controlled the lion's share of the slave trade and the profits from it, although we did not start the traffic in Africans. Subsequently, we challenged the longstanding Arab and European trade in Africans and ended it. We take the credit for this noble achievement," he stated conceitedly.

"Our tireless efforts to end the slave trade 1807 and plantation slavery after 1838, made Africa stable and productive. We must also be recognised for this too, and as a reward, for our kind-heartedness God bestowed on us another valuable opportunity, to develop trade with and colonise the African continent. Our technical knowledge and skills gave us the tools to embrace the opportunities that were plain for all to see there. Again, we exposed the abundant mineral resources of the continent, we divided the land and its wealth with our rivals to maintain peace and stability. The Negroes and Africa profited from the paid work they got from digging out the gold, diamonds, copper, platinum and the wealth of minerals all over the region. Above ground, on its never-ending and fertile plains, we cultivated cash crops for sale and our own use. The tea, coffee and cocoa plantations in Ghana, Kenya, Tanzania and Uganda to name a few," the aristocrat pointed out smugly.

"In return, Africa got the cutting-edge technology it needed, the male population learnt new skills, we taught them our language so that they could talk to each other, we built schools for those who wanted it, and our missionaries eagerly imparted the civilising words of Christianity and gave them our Bible. Selflessly, we have worked in the interest of the African continent and its people. Today, we continue to work tirelessly to benefit Africa and its population. God is our judge," he declared solemnly.

Then he left the heated arena.

I, Anancy, Ananse son of the Sky God Nyame, vigorously dispute and challenge this perverted and Eurocentric account of African history as presented by the heirs of the former enslavers. It demonstrates the much-used phrase in the islands and the mainland 'to tell Anancy story'. This expression has rightly or wrongly, evolved to describe circumstances or stories that are often laughed at and not taken too seriously. European world history is another form of 'Anancy story'. It is a gross distortion that misrepresents the historical past, by those who have profited from the enslavement and labour of Africans and other nations for centuries, on the African coastline, in the islands, the mainland of the Americas and many other regions of the world.

Between twelve and fifteen million Africans were violently snatched from their homeland. They were packed into the minuscule holds of caravels and galleons and forcibly transported to the 'Recently Enslaved World', in North, South America and the islands of the Caribbean. Significant numbers of them perished because they refused to continue the enforced journey. Thousands died because they fought their captors, and experienced the noblest reward, death at sea before reaching the planters' cane pieces.

Alarmed by the anguish and destruction inflicted on his people and continent by their theft; Nyame, the Sky God, hurled Africa's web, five times the strength of steel to the four corners of the earth. The steely web anchored his floundering and frightened children. It nurtured and soothed them in the safety of its sturdy, and silky threads. It gave them a little time and space to recover, re-orientate and rejuvenate themselves. The strength and versatility of I, Anancy, Ananse his resourceful son inspired and gave hope to his disorientated sons and daughters in whichever part of the earth they found themselves. Our insightful culture and civilisation had encapsulated elements of its worldview, in the smallest of species - an arachnid with powers to change and transform itself into a man or spider.

My unfortunate family members lodged the Spiderman and woman deep into their hearts and consciousness, during their journey to the 'Recently Enslaved World' and beyond over the centuries. Wherever, they landed they fixed the wisdom of the spider's web, along with the stories and culture of their motherland deep into the fabric of the societies they were entering. Many waited for the time and opportunity to return to their distant homeland, families and animals.

CHAPTER 2

Emancipation – what next?

Jubilantly, brothers and sisters, the Africans had fled from the sugar and coffee plantations, after August 1838 to set up small holdings of their own. Imagine, by 1860, twenty-two years after their emancipation, there were more than fifty thousand freeholders in Jamaica alone. Significant numbers of our family members had also bought land in Antigua, Barbados, Carriacou, French Guiana, Guyana, St Vincent, Grenada and Trinidad making them freeholders too. The plantation owners and the Kings and Queen of England kept the most fertile and productive lands, thus reducing the quantity and quality of land available to the free Africans. However, these enterprising people bought what they could afford in the hilly, mountainous and coastal areas of the islands and the mainland. Now, a significant number of free persons were in control of their lives and could work to benefit themselves, their families and communities. Some Africans had achieved their greatest wish, to regain their former free status, and be masters of their own destiny.

Those who could not afford to buy land left the plantations and moved to the newly created free villages to be autonomous and have some control over their future. Unfortunately, the free villages' farming lands were very limited and chiefly infertile thus limiting the ability of the landless Africans to work for themselves. The lack of productive land meant that these Africans had to remain on the plantations and take whatever wage was offered.

Regrettably, the freeholders, landowners were unable to employ their landless brothers and sisters on a large-scale. In keeping with the racial hierarchy at that time, the African freeholders and taxpayers did not have representation in the islands and the mainland's assemblies. These freeholders were prevented, from becoming members of the legislatures and participating in the governance of the country because of their race, and because it was very costly. This would affect the freeholders and workers terribly in the future. The planter-dominated legislative body governed and imposed many taxes on everyone, including all the newly freed people. Total power remained in the hands of the plantation owners, who controlled and dominated the islands and the mainland's ruling assemblies.

Unfortunately, most of our family members, more than two hundred thousand could not afford to buy land in Jamaica or in the other islands and the mainland after they had freed themselves, so they continued to work in the cane fields for meagre wages. They were bound to the sugar estates; thus, their future was extraordinarily precarious and gruelling. These landless workers would disproportionately bear the impact of natural disasters, war, downturns in the sugar economy, and the recruitment of foreign labour which increased unemployment, as the African population grew. The land issue had been critical, for all the enslaved peoples because their land was taken from them, the enslaved Taino and African peoples had worked non-stop on the enslavers' estates without wages. My kinfolk always knew from their enslavement that land was the key, they had collectively owned property in Africa, access to farmland was their insurance against the greed of the enslavers and an uncertain future.

During slavery, access to their small house plots had given the enslaved people a little control over their lives, it had given them a small amount of financial independence too. They had used their mini house plots and provision grounds in the hilly and mountainous landscape, to grow food to supplement their meagre rations and sell the surplus in the thriving Sunday markets, to buy what they could not produce. They had been exploited beyond imagination during slavery. After emancipation, wage labour on the plantations was even more horrendous, as those who did not own land had no choice, but to continue to work in the cane pieces, for whatever the cane piece owners paid them. Now, they had no direct access to land to grow food to supplement their very inadequate wages and save something for a rainy day.

The changes after emancipation, in 1838 were very minor for the majority of African workers, except for the fact that they were free, and they had to be paid for their work. However, their earnings were just above the wage the planters had not paid them during their enslavement. They were still subjected to brutal treatment by the overseers, agents and plantation holders in the cane pieces. Their minuscule wages were not sufficient to pay their rent, buy food, clothes, healthcare and schooling for their children.

The plantation owners were resentful because they had to pay wages, to the cane piece workers after the abolition of slavery in the British colonies. Their rock-bottom payments to the workers had not made them joyful. Instead, they were extremely antagonistic towards them, even though they had received 20 million pounds collectively, in today's money from the British Parliament as compensation to free the enslaved people. This substantial reward had not stopped them from wanting to maintain an indirect form of slavery on their plantations. The tightfistedness of the former enslavers towards the free Africans, grew as their freedom threatened, their economic and political dominance in the world. The planters were very concerned because the slave-owning nations of Europe continued to use slave labour on their plantations, they were suffering from unfair competition.

The labour of the Africans was vital to the plantation owners, who wanted to maintain their cane fields and profits, as well as their economic and political dominance in the world, without too much disruption. The slave economy had made the British the undisputed rulers of the world. They controlled the raw materials from their colonies, in India, North America, and Australasia, the bodies of the slaves, finance to trade and develop new industries; and a navy and army to assert their political and economic power, throughout the islands, the mainland and the world.

The plantation owners had robbed the enslaved peoples of their freedom and labour for centuries, so why would they change their attitudes towards them and promote their development after they had emancipated themselves? As you would expect, the profit-driven cane piece proprietors abandoned the free Africans after their liberation and paid the workers the smallest possible wage. The freed people provided, housing, health care and schooling for themselves as best as they could until events outside their control, and the continued negligence of the colonial administration threatened their day-to-day survival.

Bizarrely, in the fast-changing and cut-throat financial world of the time, the British government and planters pursued three significant strands in their economic policy. They were minimal pay for the African workers, the ending of the slave trade and plantation slavery by the European countries still using slave labour and the importation of indentured labourers for their plantations. These policies caused considerable economic hardships for the newly waged African workforce, and in the long term may have reduced the government and planter's own wealth creation. The new workers were penalised by these policies, even though the plantation owners admitted that their ex-slaves were the best workers, to make the smooth transition from unpaid slave labour to paid work in their cane fields. Predictably, the island's assembly and the cane piece owners refused to pay the African workers a living wage, corresponding to the ten hours or more a day they were expected to work in the cane pieces. In keeping with their past practices, the plantation owners paid the African workers a pittance for their backbreaking labour and excessive hours of work in their cane pieces.

The workers demanded more wages, the planters told them that they would pay them whatever they liked. Subsequently, the British government used the money that would have given the workers a living wage; to attempt to end the slave trade 1807 and slavery after 1838, as well as importing indentured servants from their colonies and other places to work on the plantations. The importation of workers to the plantations of the Americas allowed the plantation owners to use a divide and rule strategy, to keep wages low and prevent workers from coming together to bargain for higher wages and better working conditions. The newly paid workers rightly feared that their jobs would be taken by the imported indentured labourers; their fears were justified because downturns in the economy meant that the African worker would be the first to lose his or her job.

The British government's attempts to end the slave trade after 1807 and slavery after Emancipation in 1838, in the European colonies still using slave labour, would seem as if they were finally taking responsibility for their past actions. They had been the chief suppliers of slaves to the European territories, from 1713 until the abolition of the British slave trade in 1807. Their attempts to finally end the slave trade and plantation slavery, after 1838, must be examined objectively, because at the same time they kept their labour force in dire poverty, by refusing to pay them a wage that reflected the work and hours they expected them to do.

However, their contradictory policies and practices could be accounted for by the continuing trade in and use of slave labour by the French, Dutch, Portuguese, Spanish and American colonies. The continued trade in Africans by the European countries could eventually curtail Britain's economic power and dominance in the world. It meant that British goods were more expensive than her rivals who were still using slave labour to produce sugar and other cash crops; this might threaten the British colonies' profits and wealth in the future. Therefore, it was in the economic interest of the British state and the plantocracy, to end the slave trade and the use of slave labour in all the European colonies without delay. However, it took them about sixty years after 1808 to stop the slave trade in the Americas.

Incredibly, between 1807, and 1838, respectively, it is estimated that more than two and a half million persons were stolen from Africa and sold as slaves in the islands of the Caribbean and on the American mainland. This was happening even though the British government and navy said they were committed to ending the trade by the other European nations. British Slave patrols were deployed to seize ships carrying enslaved peoples from 1808 and take them to the designated country of safety, Sierra Leone to be documented and freed. These vessels liberated roughly one hundred and sixty thousand Africans after they were stolen from their homelands. The slave trade and slavery had continued because the other European nations had not passed laws of abolition. These countries maintained the slave trade and plantation slavery because they profited enormously from it, so they fiercely resisted the British government's attempt to stop the trade and plantation slavery in their colonies. The British government could not halt the slave trade and plantation slavery immediately after 1808 and 1838, no matter how many ships and money they used to try and stop it.

Slavery was abolished in France and Denmark, ten years later in 1848, The Netherlands in 1863, North America between 1863-5, Portugal in 1869, Spain's colony Cuba in 1886 and Brazil in 1888. To maintain its dominant economic position, as a world power, Britain had to end the continuing slave trade and plantation slavery by France, The Netherlands, Spain, Portugal and the American South after 1838. The British plantation owners kept the cane field workers' pay at a very low-level, to compete with the other colonies still trading in and using slave.labour to maintain their profits, wealth and power. The employees' low wages subsidised Britain's attempts to stop the continued slave trade and slavery after 1838. It could be argued that the total abolition of the slave trade and slavery after 1838, was paid for by the African workforce in the British colonies.

The next major blow to my kinfolk's well-being and financial aspirations was the importation of indentured servants once again, this time from the British Empire and colonies to work in the cane fields, after 1838. Before abolition, the plantation owners had convinced themselves, that the free Africans would gratefully remain in their cane pieces to work for them. Some proprietors had tried very hard to keep the about to be released Africans on their plantations, these calculating owners promised them modest rents, more significant house plots, health care by the plantation doctors, and many other benefits.

More than fifty thousand of my brothers and sisters in Jamaica did not believe the former enslavers, they fled from the plantations to total freedom, they would not be wage slaves. They bought land and had some control over their lives. As a result, their flight from the plantations had shocked, vexed and nearly crippled the plantation owners. The government and the estate owners contracted indentured workers after 1838. Firstly, they were recruited from Europe - Madeira, Scotland, Germany, Ireland and later Africa, but these workers could not revive the declining sugar production on the plantations. Subsequently, more indentured workers were recruited from within the Empire - India, to fill the gap left by the fleeing Africans. Later, more were imported from China and Indonesia to stem the decline in sugar production. The plantations reflected the British Empire, at that time and nearly all the world's population.

Imagine the cost of importing and contracting labour for the plantations, by the British government and cane piece owners. The British government paid the return fares of the contracted labourers at the end of their five to ten-year contracts if they wanted to return to their countries of origin, while the planters paid their wages and other expenses. The reality was that the imported workers did not know or have experience, of working on large scale sugar and coffee plantations. So, these workers had to learn how to work on them; thus, it took many years before sugar production rose in the cane pieces. Therefore, it would have been more advantageous to the planters and government to pay the landless workers a fair and just wage; the wages they had negotiated for instead of crushing them financially. However, they did the opposite, they imported more and more labour from the empire, this policy threatened the African workers' job and physical survival as the years passed.

The planters and the colonial government's pay policy prevented the development of a prosperous and independent African peasantry, to compete with them and drive-up labour costs. The former slave owners' policies and practices created and maintained the Africans' precarious economic and social status in the islands, the mainland and in the rest of the world. Their policies produced an army of cheap labour, which could be exploited to keep wages low and resulted in a labour force, that was permanently on the breadline. This labour force could be utilised whenever it suited them.

The planters' divide and rule strategy kept the African workers' wages static for almost a hundred years. Recession, civil war in the Southern States of America and natural disasters would further threaten their already low and stagnant pay and worsening living conditions. By 1870, three decades before the end of the century, Britain and some slave-owning countries were still arguing about putting an end to the slave trade on land and sea. The landless Africans' wages in the cane fields and elsewhere barely rose in a hundred years. So, my ambitious and hard working brothers and sisters were forced, to move between the islands and the mainland seeking improved pay and living conditions. After 1838, migration for work outside their birthplace was seen by many workers as the solution to their abject poverty, it would become the landless Africans' way out of extreme poverty in their adopted home, as the years passed. They went to Panama to construct the railway, to the banana plantations of Costa Rica and Cuba, and later some returned to Panama to build the canal. Some went to the oil fields of Venezuela, Aruba, and Trinidad as well as other islands with strong economies seeking work. They looked out from their modest dwellings at the world beyond, as the workplaces that would give them the financial liberation they so desperately wanted.

Meanwhile, living conditions worsened for the mass of workers who stayed at home, due to the fiscal turmoil in and outside the islands and the mainland. The African workforce shrank in the cane fields because the imported indentured workers replaced them. In 1865, twenty-seven years after Emancipation, these landless workers could no longer endure the hardships, that had become their everyday reality. Emancipation had not brought the improvements they had expected. A substantial section of the African population was effectively jobless, those who had work were working for less than a shilling a day. The land-owning Africans also suffered, they experienced droughts, hurricanes, taxation and the rising price of foodstuff and everyday items, they began to find it hard to feed themselves and their families too.

The island's income, its imports and exports shrunk because of the American Civil War, from 1861 to 1865, which attempted to end slavery in the Southern states of America. The economic and trading systems of the islands and the American cotton plantations were interwoven. The prices of everyday necessities increased as the American civil war created shortages in the islands because of the Northern government's blockade of the Southern states resulting in price rises. The cost of sugar fell due to competition from overseas producers, therefore reducing the need for workers. Natural disasters such as hurricanes and droughts had an impact on the plantations, and further, cut jobs and the living standards of the African masses. The colonial assembly increased duties and taxation to maintain its revenues; the African and imported labourers were paying more taxes, they were indirectly funding the war in the southern states of America, they were living in extreme poverty.

The poor and jobless workers took to the streets of their parishes and demanded help from the Governor and the Assembly to ease their distress. The landless workers of St Ann protested and wrote to the queen, governor and assembly requesting crown lands at low rents, to farm to feed themselves because the free villages did not have sufficient acreage to farm. The governor and the Queen refused, the governor told the workers to go back to the plantations and take whatever work and pay they were offered. The cane pieces were their future.

Governor Eyre, the island's governor at the time blamed the workers for their destitution and told them that their idleness and inability to work hard had caused their distress. He ordered them to work harder and defended the meagre wages they were paid. He also told them to look after themselves, it was not his or the queen's responsibility to take care of them. They must stand on their own two feet. Many of the landowning Africans were also affected by drought, hurricanes, increased taxes, and the rising cost of everyday essentials, they could not pay their taxes, so they were taken to court. The jobless workers scavenged on abandoned estates looking for food, the police arrested them and took them to court. Once again, the Africans united against those they viewed as the cause of and were indifferent to their suffering. The community leaders encouraged them to continue to express their grievances to the assembly, the queen and government.

The distressed populace discussed their complaints in their churches and gathering places, St Thomas was one of the poorest parishes on the island. Paul Bogle, deacon of a local Baptist Church at Stony Gut, in the parish of St Thomas in the East, looked for a solution. He led a group of workers and citizens to meet Governor

Eyre, in Spanish Town, the capital of the island, to tell him of the population's condition; the governor refused to meet them. The workers and freeholders stood together, as they had done in 1831 with Deacon Sam Sharp a Baptist preacher, in what became known as the Baptist War, Christmas Rebellion or Western Rebellion, that had brought an end to their enslavement. The British Government and the planters had blamed the Baptist church and its leaders for inciting the rebellion in 1831. Once again, the population would have to face their colonial masters collectively to address the injustices and neglect they suffered, as they had done during slavery.

Again, Deacon Paul Bogle walked from Stony Gut, in St Thomas in the East with his fellow Africans, to support those charged with minor offences at Morant Bay's courthouse. The British army fired and killed seven protestors, as they moved towards the building demanding that their grievances must be heard. The enraged protesters attacked the courthouse and set it on fire, a total of twenty-five people was killed, including those in the courthouse.

Governor Eyre, behaved as the planters and British administration had done during the slave rebellions. He took revenge on the already impoverished population, the militia shot five hundred of them, flogged six hundred and burned their homes. George William Gordon, also a Baptist and an elected member of the Legislature for St Thomas in the East, and a zealous supporter of his constituents was arrested and hanged, even though he was not in Morant Bay at the time of the protests. George William Gordon and Paul Bogle were executed, to terrify the protesters and to stop further uprisings by the impoverished population.

The economic liberation the Africans had wanted after emancipation had not materialised, the plantocracy continued to control all aspects of the society. They did everything in their power to block the aspirations of this free and ambitious people. The freed Africans feared being re-enslaved, as some of the insecure cane field owners had talked about breaking away and joining the Southern States of America so they could return to slavery. The colonial government and cane piece owners had not changed their attitude and behaviour, towards them after 1838.

Governor Eyre's imposition of martial law and the execution of George William Gordon, a member of the Jamaican Assembly, and Paul Bogle, as well as his brutal actions against the protestors, caused an outcry in Britain. In 1865, the British Parliament set up a commission of inquiry, to examine the conditions of the population and the state of the colony. The committee recommended and put in place some policies to alleviate the people's suffering temporarily. However, the freed people's desire for equality and open governance of the colony, as well as social and economic advancement for themselves and their families were still a distant goal.

The planter dominated assembly was abolished, and the island was ruled directly from Britain as a Crown colony until independence in August 1962. The African's journey and struggles were just beginning.

Going to market after Emancipation.

Courtesy of p.montgomery@archievesfarms.com

A Negro Hut

Courtesy of p.montgomery@archievesfarms.com

Indian festival, Jamaica
Courtesy of p.montgomery@archievesfarms.com

Nature's Bounty
Courtesy p.montgomery@archievesfarms.com

Paul Bogle leader of the Morant Bay Rebellion 1865, executed for leading the rebellion by Governor Eyre. Jamaican National Hero and Pastor.

Courtesy of the Jamaica Information Service

George William Gordon National Hero- Implicated in the Morant Bay Rebellion in 1865 and executed by Governor Eyre.

Courtesy of the Jamaica Information Service

CHAPTER 3

The Africans' struggle for economic liberation continues

The islands and the mainland of the Americas were not designed for them. It was their free and forced labour that the planters had craved and exploited mercilessly during their enslavement. Slavery had constructed them as a commodity, an army of free or nominally paid workers. They would fill-in when needed and when necessary to further the colonial governments' wealth creation endeavours. Relentlessly, the Africans had sought to rid themselves of the 'free and low-wage' label inflicted on them, during and after slavery.

After Emancipation, the British government's non-existent social policies and practices entrenched poverty, ill-health, inadequate housing, education only for those who could afford it, and very limited and very poorly paid employment for the masses. This had forced many of the newly liberated people, to move within and between the islands and the mainland of the Americas, and beyond seeking a 'living' wage for their invaluable but undervalued labour. Freedom had intensified the African's drive, for economic and political liberation and self-determination.

Many of this keen and motivated workforce had sought work within the islands and elsewhere. The wages in these countries provided temporary respite from their constant periods of unemployment and under-employment in their adopted island homes. When these external sources of low-paid and temporary work ended, these workers returned home to join the mass of under waged, underemployed and unemployed workers.

Eagerly, in the first quarter of the 20th Century, a significant number of Africans grabbed another lifeline thrown to them, by the wars that had resumed in Europe. These potential soldiers viewed the 1914 and later the 1939 wars in Europe, as a way of lifting themselves out of the hardships in their homelands and prove to the colonial world, their worth as self-motivated and dynamic human beings. They would demolish the ideology of racial superiority, that had fixed their fate during slavery, and which continued to do so after Emancipation in their adopted birthplaces.

They volunteered in huge numbers to support the mother country in her time of need. However, she snubbed them, she wanted white soldiers from the old commonwealth. She would not allow black volunteer soldiers on Europe's frontline to kill and maim white soldiers, even if they were her country's enemies. The weaknesses of the white race must never be visible to the colonised peoples. The loyal black and brown volunteers had to wait until her soldiers and officers were decimated in the trenches before she allowed them to join her armies as subordinates.

The bravery, boldness and courage of the volunteer soldiers, on the frontline, during their stint in Europe, The Middle East and Africa challenged the myths the slave owners had used to justify their ancestor's enslavement. Characteristically, Britain and the European countries, as well as their war machinery shaped by class and racial profiling, humiliated the black and brown volunteer soldiers during both wars. However, despite their inadequate housing, food, clothing, degrading work, insults, brutality, lack of promotion, racism and the injustices that were a feature of their everyday experience in the combat zone, they had excelled on the battlefield. Finally, they had proved their human capacity and worth beyond a doubt, considering all the obstacles they had to overcome.

Yet, the volunteer soldiers' significant contribution and gallantry to the liberation of Europe, in 1918 and later in 1945, was only recently acknowledged by the British government, army and people because the children of the Windrush generation researched and published their relatives heroism in both wars. At the end of the wars, the courageous and skilled black and brown volunteer soldiers were promptly returned to the harshness and squalor of the colonised Caribbean. They could not stay in the mother country because they were not white. The soldiers were overwhelmed by mass unemployment, scarcity and the appalling living conditions, that they had temporarily left behind during their time on the war-torn continents. The terrible conditions they had tried to escape from were still firmly in place. The world economic recession of the 1930's, which had started in the United States of America would further reduce the meagre wages, that had sustained those who had work.

'Better must come' was the slogan of the workers and the returning volunteer soldiers. Between the years 1933 and 1938, nearly a hundred years after they had liberated themselves from slavery; again, they rose up across the islands of the Caribbean and the South American mainland and demanded increased wages, for their valuable labour. The shilling a day that had sustained them, for nearly a hundred years could no longer cover the rising cost of foodstuffs and other essentials that had increased over time.

Again, the workers demanded realistic wages for their work. They wanted a 'dollar' a day, four shillings-Tate & Lyle, the colonial government and the remaining plantation owners in Jamaica refused, they offered them a shilling more, two shillings a day and a little more for skilled workers. The workers withdrew their labour and protested. Violently, the colonial army and police, as usual, broke up their strikes and protests. During these years, workers were killed, injured and later imprisoned in St Kitts, St Vincent, St Lucia, Trinidad and Tobago, British Guyana, and Jamaica. The labour unrest also spread to Spanish-Cuba and French-Martinique where workers, also protested for more pay and withdrew their labour. The workers were angry, they wanted compensation, they demanded that the plantations be turned over to them, as compensation for the non-payment of wages to their ancestors during slavery, they believed that it had been agreed by the British monarch in 1838.

To get the maximum profit from their plantations, the enslavers had worked the enslaved peoples to death during slavery. They had promptly replaced them with a never-ending supply, of men, women and children from Africa. Colonial and Empire business interests had turned their post-Emancipation earnings, into a diminishing wage, static and microscopic payments for maximum work. After emancipation, the employers would only pay the lowest wage or no take-home pay for human work if the workers allowed them to get away with it.

The profit-driven bosses, again ignored their employee's appeals for better wages, just as they had done during slavery. Now, their descendants were forced to use the same strategies to wrench from the plantation owner's profits a fair and just wage. The workers stood together and protested against their starvation wages, and withheld their labour. The governors and planters, again behaved as they had done during slavery. Their armies and constabularies attacked and flogged the striking and protesting workers. The workers resisted, their protests and strikes increased, so the employers' and government militia, killed, injured and gaoled many of them.

The labourers had chosen the most articulate among them, as well as those who had knowledge of Britain's institutional practices and procedures to represent them. The volunteer soldiers' self-confidence had increased because of their gallantry and experiences on the battlefields of Europe, The Middle East and Africa. Now, they and their fellow workers would take control of all aspects of their lives, their islands and the mainland, as their fore parents had done during slavery to become a free and viable people.

The spokespersons for the employees negotiated with the employers for increased wages, the managers refused to negotiate and gaoled some of them. The union officials organised the workforce in their workplaces, and then into unions. As production fell and their profits started to decline significantly, the bosses gave in and negotiated with their employees' representatives. However, they would only pay the smallest possible increase in pay. The government, businesses and the planters stood firm and did not improve on their offer of a shilling. The workers got two shillings a day for their efforts. Officially, the organised labour movement in the colonised islands and the mainland of the Americas was born.

In 1940, the employees and their unions continued their demands for better pay and living conditions, they campaigned and forced the colonial government, to set up another commission to investigate the state of the people. The commission's conclusions were published in The Moyne Report 1945, at the end of the Second World War. In the meantime, the workers continued to use their skimpy wages to make ends meet until they could find other ways to improve their financial position. Soon, many of this workforce determined to transform their economic well being would be on their way to rescue the bankrupt and ailing economy of post-war Britain. However, the attitude of the mother country to her children had not changed after both wars, she was not grateful for the help they had given her to defeat the Fascist German and Italian regimes. She wanted white workers to rebuild her country after the war.

Again, the workers, peasant farmers and returning volunteer soldiers from the islands and the mainland were on the move, but they were not going back to Africa, their ancestral home. They were en route to the bombed-out urban areas of the mother country to become an exploited workforce. Desperately, the National Health Service, The Railways, London Transport and the private sector recruited them to reconstruct the crippled cities and economy reduced to rubble, by Hitler and Mussolini's bombardments, when they could not get enough white workers.

This was not the first time the African Diaspora would be directly financing the development of the United Kingdom and Europe. From the close of the 15th Century and beginning of the 16th Century, their ancestors had been enslaved and forced to work in mines, and on tobacco, sugar and coffee plantations without pay, until 1838 when they liberated themselves in the British colonies. The wealth created by their ancestors' free labour went straight to the mother country and helped to finance the industrial revolution in Britain, making her a world power with an empire. The Windrush generation and their ancestors had been continuously contributing to the wealth of the mother country, long before Caribbean migration began in 1948.

Arrogantly, the government, the ruling class and the working population of the United Kingdom refused to acknowledge their contribution, they were enormously indebted to them and their ancestors, for their forced financial gift over the centuries. Yet, those who knew and had benefited from their labour refused to recognise their input. Instead, they treated them atrociously at their arrival. The Windrush generation and their children could not, and would not recoup the billions of pounds owed to them and their ancestors by the mother country because many of them were employed in the very low paid sectors of the economy. Their combined earnings in post-war Britain, could not generate the billions of pounds the enslavers and the British government owed them and their ancestors in compensation.

Before the returning volunteer soldiers and migrants had set foot on British soil from the Empire Windrush, some government officials and citizens were exceedingly perturbed. They must not be allowed to step onto their 'Fatherland'. The ship must be redirected to Africa or returned to the islands and mainland. They did not want workers from the West Indies, Africa or Asia in their country. They had to keep Britain white.

Fortunately, for these very ambitious workers, the destroyed cities, towns and industries of the United Kingdom saved them. They were crying out for labour, they needed a sizeable and low-paid labour force, they would have them. On a cloudy morning on June 22nd, 1948, the *'Empire Windrush'* docked at Tilbury, London. The islanders and the mainlanders disembarked to guarantee the reconstruction of the mother country. In its relatively comfortable compartments below deck, were 492 eager men and one woman, many black and brown ex-service personnel from both the first and second world wars. They were returning to the United Kingdom; as well as keen islanders seeking to improve their life chances, that was first destroyed by slavery and then constrained by colonialism. The penniless female stowaway on board, carried the hopes and dreams, of many of her sisters left on the islands and the mainland to improve their, and their families' lives.

On board were citizens of the British Empire and the Black Commonwealth, Jamaica, Trinidad and Tobago, Guyana, Barbados, St Lucia and the other islands. They had sold their assets, cows, goats, pigs and family land to pay their fares to guarantee a more secure financial future for themselves and their families. As the enthusiastic, but bewildered immigrants peered through the ship's portholes at the cold, bleak and frosty unwelcoming country and population, they decided five years would be enough to achieve their financial goals. They were in love with their adopted island homes, even if the Isles had not provided the economic security to keep them there. They would return home as soon as they could. Unfortunately, they did not realise that the workplaces in Britain were not generous, they would pay them just enough to keep them working continuously until their retirement.

They were a second-choice workforce. Yet, the Africans had been the first choice of the enslavers more than four centuries before because their labour was free. If money and prestige were involved, they would always be second best, they could have the leftovers the white population did not want. They would be tolerated as long as they accepted the second-class status the society imposed on them. If some of these migrant's ancestors had fled the plantations via underground tunnels of freedom during slavery, now many of their great, great, great, grand children's first homes in the mother country would be in the underground air-raid shelters in Clapham, south London. The assistants in the Labour Exchange in Coldharbour Lane, Brixton, fiddled with and filed over and over the thousands of vacancies on their books around the country. They would have these would-be workers, even though as experienced recruiters they knew that they would not be up to the job. They would bide their time, time would prove them right.

Brixton's bombed-out streets and run-down houses accommodated many of them and became their first settlement in the mother country. Brixton would become the heartbeat and centre of the island community in London, as well as those in the other cities and towns of the United Kingdom. It would be the centre of the community's resistance, cultural, educational, community and political organisation. Others spread out across London and the other industrial cities of the United Kingdom in search of, the employment and opportunities, they had yearned for since their ancestor's enslavement and emancipation. The calypsonian, Lord Kitchener smiled and sang, "London, London, this lovely city, London is the place for me" as he stepped onto the gangway from the Empire Windrush, reassuring his alarmed hosts that they would be good citizens. They were here to earn a little money and would very soon return to the islands. The song also summed up his and his fellow passengers' hopes and dreams, as they stepped onto the soil of the mother country, from the Empire Windrush.

The islands and the mainland's elite, on board the ship would transform the suburbs of London and the regions of the United Kingdom into multi-racial and multicultural communities, for all to live and work in relative harmony in the years to come. Brothers and sisters, I will leave the stage and let my family members tell their stories, I will return later, to reflect.

Barbadians waiting to board ship for England in 1948.
Courtesy of the London transport Museum, London

Air raid shelter Clapham South, London
Photo: B Ellis

CHAPTER 4

England here we come

The children were excited, and so they danced around their mother. We are going to England they sang at the top of their voices repeatedly. We are going to England to see our father, we are going to see him in England.

'Why oonu nuh keep quiet? Mi haffi tink wha mi haffi do, oonu fadda waan wi fi come, but him nuh sen all di money. Im no hab all a it. Mi wi haffi tink wha mi a go do fi get all di money fi tek all a wi. Mi nah lef any a oonu yah. Oonu fadda lef mi wid oonu, now wi all haffi go a England together. Mi nuh waan nobody fi know yet, til mi tink wha fi do,' she told the children.

That night she tossed and turned, her problems were just beginning. Her husband had sent her a hundred pounds, but it was not enough to get her and the seven children to England, by aeroplane or ship. She could not think about borrowing anything from her neighbours. They would rightly think how could she ask them for money, when her husband was in England three years, while they were all trying hard to make ends meet.

She knew they would not understand. They believed that once you had someone in England or the United States, your money problems were over. Her husband was writing to tell her how hard it was for him there. She had looked after, her neighbour Mammie when her daughter had left for England. She had sent the old woman a little dinner each evening with one of the children. At the weekend, she would send her Sunday dinner, rice and peas with chicken, some carrot and beetroot juice, linseed or Irish moss. The old woman and her daughter were eternally grateful. The old lady would send fruit from her backyard for the children. This was how they lived in Jamaica, the islands and the mainland in those days.

When times were hard for them, and her husband could not get any work in Kingston, Mammie had asked her daughter to help them out. Her daughter had been in England for some years and gladly agreed to pay her husband's fare to England. She also offered him work in the little West Indian bakery they had set up in North London, not far from Kings Cross Station. Many Jamaicans were living in that area, they searched the streets to find their foods from back home. They bought 'hard dough' bread, patties, Easter bun and the little treats they were used to back home from the small bakery. They came from all over London and the larger towns to get 'back home' delicacies.

Her husband had to pay Mammie's daughter back each week out of his small wage, post money to her for the children, eat and pay his bills. She had made the few pounds he sent her, each month go a long way. She had expected him to send for the family after a year. But it had taken him three years to get the money together, she would have to find the rest.

Now she had to think about how she could make up the money. Her small garden plot had helped her to stretch the little funds, she received from the children's father each month. She could not grow and sell enough vegetables to make up the boat fare to England. She would have to sell the little house, they had worked on over the years to make comfortable and respectable in their small but aspiring community. Her neighbours had looked up to her. Her husband was in England, and she was bringing up their seven children on her own. The children were well-behaved and always neat and tidy. The two eldest were also doing well at the local primary school. Her daughter's teacher had told her she was preparing her for the Common Entrance exam the following year. Only last week, she had proudly told a neighbour that her eldest son had passed the Common Entrance examination and had won a scholarship to St Georges College, one of the best secondary schools in Kingston. She had worried about the books and the uniform for him, but she knew his father would be pleased.

He would be very proud of his first born, she knew he would try his best to let her have a little more money, each month to meet the new expenses. Now the issue of her sons' scholarship was no longer a problem. He would go to England and receive the best education possible; *definitely* better than he would get in Jamaica. Now, all she had to think about was selling her furniture, the house and some bits and pieces to get enough money to buy the tickets. She thought about what to do first. The furniture would not be a problem; she had always liked and wanted nice things. She had bought the latest furniture in one of the big stores down town on King Street. She had paid for it little by little until it was finished. Many people in the community would want to buy them. She had to think carefully about the house. The land was leased and may cause a problem, for anyone who bought it, if the owner wanted the land back soon.

As she walked around the yard and house the following morning, trying to work out how much she might ask for it; a friendly and gentle voice interrupted her thoughts. She turned and saw Brother Clee standing by the gate with a small basket of fruits and vegetables.

"Fah di pickney dem," he had said as he handed it over the gate to her. Graciously, she took it and remembered her dilemma. She opened the gate and invited Brother Clee in. They sat on the small veranda and looked out into the lane as their neighbours went about their business. In the distance, the church dominated the small community. Its bells rang out as if calling the residents to prayers.

"Tank yuh, Brother Clee, di pickney dem gwine like di tamarinds, an mi wi roast di breadfruit fah breakfast a mawnin."

She trusted Brother Clee. She knew her business would be safe with him. She also knew he would give her the best advice and help. When her husband had left, and she was carrying their seventh child, Brother Clee had helped her out when the baby was due. He had sent his young niece to look after the children until the mother could resume her role. He had called each evening to make sure she was managing. The mother had been grateful for his help and kindness.

Brother Clee she continued, "mi hear fram mi husband an im waan all a wi fi cum a England. But mi haffi sell di house an mi tings fi get all di money, ef all a wi fi go. I tink di house a go be a problem, people nuh hab money. Times hard fah everyone, dem nuh hab no wuk an mi waan fi go as soon as mi can."

Brother Clee smiled his gentle broad smile. Then said, "Mi happy fah yuh an di pickney dem Mistress Brown."

A gust of wind drifted by, his long and weighty matted hair swung around his broad and sturdy shoulders. His wrinkled brow and soft, kind eyes showed his delight at the news. This happy family would be reunited; not in the land of their birth but across the ocean in London, England. He was pleased, over the years he had earned her respect and the esteem of all the people who lived in their small community.

Brother Clee made furniture during the day with his boy apprentices. He had collected as many school dropouts, as he could and gave them a thorough apprenticeship in furniture making. Those boys who finished their apprenticeships with him became skilled craftsmen, and their services were sought in the community and beyond. In the evenings, he cultivated his plot of land in his backyard, just as the enslaved Africans had done during slavery to increase their inadequate rations, and to earn a little money by trading in the Sunday markets. This necessity and tradition had stayed with the freed people after their liberation. The elder kept a keen and watchful eye over all the community's children, and gently guided them in their actions.

The children skipped by his side and talked to him. Silently, they wondered why this man was so different from their fathers, uncles and brothers. Brother Clee handed small parcels of fruits and vegetables over the fences to their parents. He acted as a go-between when members of the community quarrelled with each other. This man could get the most stubborn and contentious enemies, to talk and settle their differences. He was the thread that drew and bound the small community together. He was a glowing example of human beings relating to each other positively and constructively. For all those who crossed his path, they felt this was how it should be and would be, in the transformed island, islands and the mainland that they and their ancestors before them had struggled and longed for, and had so desperately wanted after Emancipation and independence.

Up and down the island in the mountainous interior, these honest and faithful members of the community worked hard to improve the quality of life for themselves, and their communities. Brother Clee was safe in his neighbourhood, from the antagonism and disrespect shown by those groups on the island, who wanted and upheld the monetary gains, values and lifestyles of their white colonial masters. This community would protect him from their disapproval and contempt. Brother Clee's and the mass of the people's experiences were the same, the Africans made up ninety percent of the population, but still owned less than one percent or so of its wealth. Health, education, housing, rewarding job prospects and moving up in society was a distant and elusive goal that emancipation and independence had not given them. These were the descendants, of the enslaved Africans that were brought from Africa in slave galleons, and forced to work in mines, on the sugar, coffee and cotton plantations for centuries, without pay.

In 1838, the Africans had thrown off the physical chains of slavery, yet the transformation that they had hoped for in their everyday lives had not taken place. They were still very, very poor, while the white minority continued to be prosperous, and masters of the island, islands and the world. A few blacks and browns were sandwiched between extreme wealth and abject poverty, they aspired to the values and the affluence of the whites above them while despising the misery of the blacks below them. The mass of black workers had jobs now and then. Daily their families were hungry, although they had worked hard to pull themselves up out of the legacy of their ancestors' enslavement. However, they were continually plunged into the depths of despair and abject poverty, due to the deep-rooted social and economic divisions created by slavery and then colonialism.

Now, their paths crossed with their colonial masters, not as slaves but as low-paid cleaners, cooks, drivers, gardeners, plantation workers, porters, dock workers, nursemaids and washerwomen. Brother Clee and many like him had taken a different path, they rejected the monetary values and behaviour of the former enslavers and colonialists that had kept and intended to keep them, in dire poverty and dependency forever. The men and women in the hilly interior knew that the world and the islands could be different if the resources of the islands and the world were shared out more equitably among the world's population. Brother Clee and the people like him knew that continuing to, ape the ways of those that had enslaved them, would never make them financially viable and equal human beings.

Instinctively, the matted hair men and women chose alternative ways of living and relating to their fellow Africans. The traditions and culture of their ancestors and their ancestral homes in Africa were the answer to the colonial exploitation, that was imposed on them. These men and women looked to their ancestral home, Africa with its communal lifestyles, culture, relationships and practices as the model to guide their future relations with each other. They took to the hills and the undulating countryside, to escape persecution from the brown and black defenders of colonialism and the white social and monetary order. They bonded with those whose skin colour mirrored their own, in the shanty towns of the cities and the free villages of the interior and encouraged communal living, using the land their ancestors had toiled on without pay as an enslaved workforce for centuries. They celebrated their African origins and culture as much as they could, within the constraints of the colonised island, islands and the mainland. They had begun a revolution which would progressively challenge the foundations of white supremacy and culture along with its exploitative money-making practices.

This family like so many before them were on their way to London, England, a mother and her seven children, paid for by their ambitious and responsible father in England. He had escaped from the squalor and pain of the island in 1961, before political independence to guarantee his children's future, a future that had been denied to him and many others in the islands and mainland. The British Nationality Act of 1948, had given every Commonwealth citizen, British subject status, three years after World War II ended.

The Act was designed to give citizenship and jobs to white Commonwealth and displaced European workers only. The authors of the Act had envisioned a white labour force, but they could not recruit them. Reluctantly, and under pressure and censure from the colonies in the Americas, Africa and Asia the policy of white only recruitment was abandoned. The pool of destitute labour from the Black Commonwealth would be mobilised to fill the gap, overall they would be much cheaper too. Accidentally, and fortunately for the islanders, the mainlanders, and the Indian sub-continent, the 1948 Act, had rightly provided citizenship and entry for all the mother country's children black and white. This begun the recruitment of migrants from the islands, the mainland and the Indian sub-continent to work in the United Kingdom from the early 1950s. However, roughly a decade later in 1962 controls on immigration began to be tightened as the white population squealed at the number of black workers entering the country. The 1962 Act restricted the numbers of immigrants coming into Britain, except for their dependants and those with permission to enter and seek work from the non-white commonwealth.

CHAPTER 5

The Journey

The pristine and turquoise coastal waters, of the Caribbean Sea, merged gently into the dark blue of the Atlantic Ocean; as massive see-sawing waves and tides hurled the ship towards Europe's Northern shoreline. Icy winds whistled across its bubbling and water-logged sundecks. Terrified and trembling the children clung to the makeshift rope railings, that had stopped the raging ocean from casting them into its frothy underbelly forever. Rapidly, another enormous wave chucked itself at the ship's bow, the bow heaved and threw them uncontrollably into the cold foaming waters. Desperately, they clung to the rigid ropes that were in place to regulate the boisterous ocean.

Gingerly, the white-clad crew led the subdued, soaked and shivering children below deck to the safety and security of their mother's cabin. Sternly, the tubby Italian seamen warned her in their Italian-English accents, to keep them from the upper decks of the ship, until the turbulent sea had calmed itself. The youngsters wondered how long they would be imprisoned, in their mother's cabin eating rice, corn beef and stinking boiled cabbage.

The family was on the second stage of the triangular journey, but this time the cargo was not sugar, molasses, rum or cocoa to be sold to augment the profits, of British merchants, bankers, the nobility and governments. Instead, these ships now carried the descendants of, skilled men, women and their children to operate the buses, factories, offices, restaurants, and hospitals of the large cities and towns of the United Kingdom. They would be paid whatever their bosses felt they could give them while making a splendid profit. The children's three-week journey had made them, and their lone parent long for the calm of the land they were migrating to.

The violent rocking of the ship gradually eased, the hazy sun peeped through the portholes at them now and then. The youngsters were comforted, that their ordeal was coming to an end. Expectantly, they stared out from the cabin's small round windows and saw calm blue waters stretching into the distance peacefully. Goosebumps covered their bony black arms, as they shivered and shuddered uncontrollably, they wanted their journey across the wild Atlantic Ocean to end. Their adventure had been spoilt by the ocean's rowdy antics.

The battered ship edged its way towards the white cliffs of Southampton docks, leaving behind the gigantic frothy white waves that had curtailed the youths' exploration of the nook and crannies of the ocean liner. On a crisp and chilly November day, the hazy sun, straggled the upper and lower decks, as the sailors prepared the ship for disembarkation. It seemed as if the intermittent sunshine was welcoming the passengers to their new country. The children pressed their noses onto the blurry portholes, to catch a glimpse of the place that had separated them from their absent parent; while the frothy sea gave way to powdery white walls, that seemed to stretch beyond the ship as far as they could see.

New terrors engulfed them, the whiteness beyond the portholes alarmed them. They moved away from the cabin's round windows, hoping this would banish the anxieties welling-up inside them. They drew closer and closer to their mother for protection from the never-ending white barrier that seemed to enclose the ship. They clung to her to get past the whiteness that now frightened them, and which would possibly limit their escapades in the new country, they were about to enter.

Patiently, the children waited with their lone parent to leave what had been their temporary home for weeks, the white-walled terrors beyond the ship's deck had subdued them. Cautiously, they edged forward holding onto their mother's skirt, confidently their fellow passengers strode towards the gangway, to embrace this cold, mysterious land and whatever the future had in store for them. It was unlike their ancestors' experience more than four hundred years before, when the enslaved peoples', feet were rooted to the floor of the galleons. Reluctantly, they had been prodded and shoved from the ships' decks onto the hot and gleaming white sandy beaches of the islands and the mainland, to be auctioned off and enslaved for their labour.

The family were left behind in the commotion, as the hopeful workers rushed towards immigration and their waiting family and friends outside. Slowly and apprehensively, the youngsters hauled their luggage, to help the family's exit to the unknown white landscape that now intimidated them. They ambled towards the desk, the eager passengers had left. The bright pink face of the immigration officer startled them. Fortunately, he ignored them and peered into the face of their mother, then beckoned to their tallest sibling to come forward with his protruding chin. The officer scrutinised him closely, said nothing, and returned the passport, then steered the mother and her brood away from him, again with his extended chin. The mother coaxed the children to keep up with the stragglers from their ship, hurrying to the lounge containing the reassembled passengers; their eagerness curtailed by their missing families and transport.

A sea of black faces filled the waiting room, they had returned to Jamaica. Diligently, the family without a father searched the room for the face they felt they had forgotten, in the intervening years. They did not know their dad. Was he one of the tall, short, medium height men who busied themselves searching the room for relatives? One by one their fellow travellers attached themselves to a welcoming party. The children continued to look into the dwindling countenances for their parent, soon there were only a few men left in the room that could be their father. They were alone, again with their mother. Had he forgotten them, or better still had he abandoned them in this frosty land where steam was now curling into the air from inside their bodies?

Their hopes rose once more, as a tall man came towards them, almost swallowed up by his long black overcoat. They wanted him to be their father, they liked his dress and appearance. Their mother didn't stir, she looked past him for the features of her husband. He wasn't their father. Suddenly, the man spoke to their lone parent and asked where they were going, he explained that it was getting late and the service would be closing very soon, as no more ships were expected. He told the family that their ship was not due to dock until the following day, it had arrived a day early, the workers had come in to unload the vessel and would want to go home to their families.

He had driven to the docks, when he was not working, to help his country people who might be travelling alone or were stranded for whatever reason. He always found travellers needing help, this large family needed his help. He invited them to join him and some of their fellow passengers in his minivan going to London. As the small van whizzed through the tranquil English countryside, the children saw rows and rows of joined-up houses, partly linked houses and some with land around them like the home they had left behind in Kingston. They hoped that when they were eventually reunited with their missing father, the family would have a big house with land around it. Living in England would be fun, if they lived in a large house, then they could put up with the cold weather that had penetrated their flimsy cotton clothes, making them shiver and shake, they were freezing.

The van stopped in all kinds of streets, narrow and wide ones. Some had beautiful houses with big gardens around them, as well as small streets with worn flat-fronted dwellings, scruffy shops and no yards. Their fellow passengers exited and were greeted enthusiastically by their family and friends, in no time the van was empty except for the family without a father. Their good Samaritan named the places as he stopped to let off his passengers, Harlesden, Willesden, Cricklewood and Neasden, the family listened eagerly but did not recognise the names. Then, he told them they were in North West London now, South London was next, but it would take about half an hour if the traffic were flowing. They sat bolt upright when the driver told them they were in South London, they were curious, their father lived somewhere in these streets. Then, he informed them they were very near, as he drove along Denmark Hill, the van halted, and waited to turn, they sensed they were near their new home and their father.

The children had looked approvingly at the substantial houses set back from the road with lawned front gardens on Denmark Hill, they had failed to notice some of the older and shabbier buildings and homes along the street too. A sizeable house like these would make up for the disappointment of their missing father, and the cold that was freezing their fingers and toes they told themselves. Finally, they were on the road of their father.

As the van drove along Herne Hill Road, their eyes darted from right to left to find their new home. They were disappointed that the houses got smaller, much smaller than the ones they had seen on Denmark Hill, some were linked up residences with small front gardens. However, they were encouraged that it was still a pleasant looking road. It had some houses which looked as if they had many rooms even if they were joined together with smoke curling into the air from pots on their roofs. The van stopped outside a flat fronted house with three floors in a row of linked houses. They had tiny front gardens.

The children looked up at the three-storey house, it was tall and impressive from the outside; but they were very disappointed with the garden, they wondered if the house had a big backyard. It would do they thought, as they returned to thinking about their absent father. They waited inside in the van, while the driver rang the doorbell and waited. A short, plump, light-skinned woman answered the door. The aroma of rice and peas and chicken escaped and sailed through the door into the hallway, and into the van. The scent of back home cooking comforted the children and made them smile.

The driver opened the van's door, they got out. He led them into the long narrow entrance hall of the house, where the delicious smell of the meal lingered. Instantly, they banished the smell of the stinking cabbage from the ship. Again, the wife looked for her husband and the children's father. Then she asked the woman about her husband. The woman invited them in and told her that she thought Mr Brown had gone to work today. She had not seen or heard him.

"Im a wuk on a Sunday to," asked the wife incredulously.

"Yes," she said. "Im wuk all hours di good Lord sen fi look afta im fambly."

"Wi is his fambly. Wi reach Southampton an expect im fi meet wi," she said agitatedly.

The kind-hearted woman invited them into her ground floor apartment, it was not huge, but it was not small either. The smell of rice and peas comforted them and banished their disappointment. They felt at home. The children sat on the edges of a sofa, chairs, in all the free places they could find with plates on their laps. The woman left the room and returned with a pot. She piled small mounds of rice and peas, a slice of tomato and gravy smelling of seasoned chicken on their little plates. She apologised for the small portions, explaining that she had not expected visitors. Next, she offered them paper cups with carrot juice. The woman's young sons scowled and watched the children eat, they would make sure those hungry kids would not come again to eat their food.

England was just like Jamaica the kids thought, people ate rice and peas for Sunday dinner. However, in Jamaica, they would have had more significant portions of chicken and rice, and a big yard to run about in afterwards to rid themselves of their excess energy. As they waited for their father to arrive, the children eyed each other up, the newly arrived children wondered if they would be their playmates. Where would they play together? They could not see a big yard outside, they imagined their play space would be the small front garden, their garden in Jamaica was much bigger and better.

They consoled themselves that it was good to be in England, they would be with their mother and father now, and the food was the same as in Jamaica, but they preferred the yard of their Kingston home. The family waited patiently for their father to come home from his long work day. Now, they understood what their mother had said about working hard at school, and always doing their best. Their father was at work today, the day of their arrival, he had gone to work on Sundays in the cold, rain, and snow to send money to feed and school them. They would work hard in school, like their father in his workplaces to make him proud of them. The parents would instil the work ethic in their children.

Caribbean men arriving at Southampton Dock 1963

Courtesy of Howard Grey 1962

Women arriving at the station from the West Indies

Courtesy of Howard Grey 1962

Herne Hill Road

Photo: B Ellis

CHAPTER 6

The reunion

The absent parent had decided not to work too late today, after all, it was Sunday. He would go home and rest for the long journey to the dock in the morning, to get his family. Uncle John would pick him up at 5 am, to avoid running into too much traffic. He could always count on Uncle John for help when he needed it. He worked with him at the building firm, officially he was the driver that brought the materials to the men on the job. When they worked outside London, for example in Slough, the company would hire a van, and Uncle John would pick up the workers and take them to the site. Although the driver was much younger than him, he always asked him for advice, Uncle John knew his way around. The driver and painter had come to England in 1958, from Jamaica, and had paid a deposit on a big three-storey house in West Dulwich some years later, which his sister and her family shared with him. He would become a close family friend as the years passed.

Mr Brown had always wanted to learn to drive and buy a car, so he could pick up his family and take them around when they arrived from Kingston. But he had spent every penny he earned paying for the room he rented in Stockwell, the rest went to his children back home, fed him and paid his fare to and from work. Now, that he had found a larger place for the family, he was spending even more of his small wages. The painter always had employment, he was a good worker, and his employer appreciated his thoroughness. He painted each house, flat, factory or bridge with due care and attention.

So, when the employee asked the foreman for some extra work, the foreman was happy to give it to him. He could trust Mr Brown to do a good day's work without supervision. The father turned the key in the lock, the door opened. Instinctively, he walked towards the stairs, when Mrs Cann called him into her apartment. Her wide grin puzzled him. He had always called out to her from the hallway but had not entered her flat. Her husband was a quiet man, Mr Cann kept himself to himself. She seemed to be the male and female of the house. He was wary of such women. He entered the apartment and saw many eyes staring up at him, he did not immediately recognise all the faces.

"Dem cum," Mr Brown. "Tree hours ago, mi give dem a lickle rice an peas dat's all mi hab. Dem is yours now." Swiftly, Mrs Cann ushered them out of her flat.

The parent guided his wife and children up the narrow stairway, looking back to see if they were managing, but also taking every opportunity to see if he could recognise all their faces and remember all their names. The family stopped on the next floor expecting to be shown into the rooms. The parent beckoned them up another flight of stairs to the top of the house where it was light and inviting. Proudly, he turned to his expectant family and told them that this was their flat and new home. They entered a large square shaped room with a cooker, fridge and sink behind the door, the rest of the space had a table, a sofa and some chairs. A huge window faced the kitchen behind the door.

"This is the living room he informed them. The two other rooms are bedrooms."

He showed them the gas and electric metres on the landing and a small storage area. Next to the storage area was the parents' bedroom.

"The toilet is on the floor below, and the bathroom is on the ground floor next to Mrs Cann's kitchen and flat," he told them.

The children thought the apartment was a lot smaller than their house in Kingston, and what they had hoped for on their journey from the docks. Nevertheless, they would be living in a big house with three floors in England. Their missing father had painted the rooms in the most cheerful and stylish colours. So, although the flat was small for such a big family, the rooms were bright, pleasing and welcoming as their well looked after house in Jamaica. Then, he showed his wife and children the rest of the flat and fed them from the fridge. He took bread, ham and margarine from the refrigerator and buttered bread and made sandwiches to supplement their previous meal. They ate, and the parents prepared them for bed. They slept soundly on their first night in England, knowing all would be well now that they had found their absent father, and they would all be together.

The honking of car horns and fast-moving traffic outside their bedroom window woke them. Slowly, they got up, stretched and pulled back the curtains and peered out of the window. They saw nothing, steam gushed from their mouths and nostrils onto the already milky window pane. They trembled and shivered as the cold air in their bedroom nipped at their faces and fingers. The view from the window was the same as the scene from the porthole of the ship's cabin. They wiped the glass, but that made it even frostier than before. They gave up looking out of the window for the time being. The youngsters scrambled about trying to manage their new surroundings, they dressed in the clothes their father had laid out for them in their bedroom.

Curious to learn about their new surroundings, they attempted to look out of the bedroom window for a second time, with difficulty they could just make out the grey misty morning, slowly giving way to beams of sunlight as the sun struggled to rise and warm, the bleak November day. The bustle of women and children intrigued them, the women dressed in dark clothing pushed little metal carts with something inside, while the younger kids held onto the sides of the wagon, the older ones walked ahead, looking back at intervals. The hectic to and froing held their interest for some time, soon this would be their routine.

When they entered the living room, dressed in over-sized winter clothes, they found their mother alone by the stove. Once again, their father was missing. He had left before daylight for his painting assignment in a London borough. However, she assured them that he would be with them the following day to show them around, and seek out schools for them. They were in an unfamiliar house, in a cold and frosty country with their mother, but they felt safe huddled together in front of the cooking and paraffin stoves. He had left treats for them, the smell of an 'English breakfast' had filled the room and their nostrils. The smell of eggs and bacon being prepared was so different from their back-home breakfasts. He had left black tea with milk, lashings of margarine and white bread with bacon and eggs for them to eat as much as they wanted.

The children were delighted with their English breakfast, they would no longer be sent at the crack of dawn to pull bushes such as mint, cerasee or soursop leaf from trees, shrubs and fences behind the house to put into pots of boiling water, to make their tea before school. They had not decided yet if they were lucky or unlucky at having been spared the chore of collecting their breakfast each morning. No longer, would they have to go around the watercourse cutting callaloo to be steamed for breakfast with boiled or fried dumplings. Some mornings, it had been boiled bananas taken from the bending trees, or roast breadfruit that had recently fallen or picked from the enormous spreading tree in the backyard. Sometimes, the older children would be spared the task of collecting their breakfast, because a neighbour or neighbours had brought their mother breadfruit, green or ripe bananas, callaloo and various bushes to make their tea and morning meal.

In England, it was all done for you, they knew that unlike back home going out to collect your breakfast on a cold frosty morning would not be fun, even if you were wrapped up in the warmest clothes. They had not seen any fruit trees that would provide food for their breakfast or school snacks. There were no banana, pawpaw, mango, orange or sweetsop trees or freshly grown vegetables from their mother's vegetable plot in the backyard. From now on, their food would be bought from the local shop, or beforehand at a supermarket or in Brixton market if they wanted food from back home. This was how people lived in England, and they would have to get used to it. Everything was packaged, dried or frozen for their parents' convenience, all they had to do was to work and pay for it.

There was no space to grow anything, even if they wanted to. The kids had seen the backyard of the three-storey house, it was small and concreted over with some dried-up plant stalks in a huge pot. Across the way, the trees were all dead, with no leaves or fruits on any of them. Back home almost all the trees were green, with colouring from the lightest to the darkest green with a variety of patterned leaf shapes to match, and they all gave fruit, even if you could not eat them. That evening their father came home from work early. Night came quickly in November, they dreaded leaving their home. Few persons moved in the streets now, except for silhouettes walking to work or home.

Searchingly, they looked at their handsome father, desperately trying to remember actions or events they had shared. The older ones recalled, the Friday evenings when their tall and good-looking father had ridden his bicycle along the sandy and dusty lane home, bringing their favourite chocolate ice-cream cake. They recalled the man who mended fences and sand-dashed their house to make it stand out in the small but aspiring community. He had dug up the vegetable patch so their mother could grow vegetables. He had been a quiet and reserved father, and they could not recall any disagreements between them.

However, they remembered their mother's threats to tell their father about their bad behaviours. His stern looks were enough to ensure they did as they were instructed. They would not miss out on the Friday evening treats. The youngsters were enjoying the honeymoon, they would also try hard not to do anything to upset their parents because there was no backyard to hide in, or under house cellar to spend all day until your parents had forgotten the misdemeanours. The next morning, they woke early as the smell of the paraffin stoves warmed the cold rooms, and steamed up the windows blocking their view of the outside world yet again.

The smell of bacon and eggs once again filled the small apartment. They shared their 'English breakfast' with both parents. They ate their favourite breakfast with lashings of toasted white bread and butter washed down with black tea, milk and sugar, until they were full. The father looked on approvingly as his family ate and enjoyed the breakfast he had prepared for them.

"Let them enjoy these precious moments", he thought.

Soon they would be trudging through the rain and snow, in smog-filled London, daily their fingers and toes would freeze from the cold air around them. The carefree fun-filled days back home were over for all of them. The oldest children promptly became their parents' little helpers, as the mother would have to work too. They were still very young, not teenagers yet but they would learn quickly. The girl was ok, she had been her mother's helper when he was away in England. She would adapt to her new role in England. Both parents would have to work to provide the very best for their seven children. Their children would get the best education they could get for them. Education was the future, and everyone in the community knew this, they had seen their neighbours and close family members' children succeed and become confident members of their communities with good jobs.

They had migrated to get work and education for their children, steady employment was all they had wanted and schooling for their children. However, work had been elusive, you had to know people to get a little work, and if you got work, it would be daily, and the pay would not be enough to look after your family. England would give them the opportunity to work and take care of their families, their utmost desire in the islands and the mainland since their ancestors liberated themselves in 1838.

In Jamaica, as soon as the boy and girl were old enough, he had sent them to Mrs Scott's basic school. They had paid a shilling a week for each child, they could not afford it, but it meant his wife had to grow more flowers and vegetables to sell on Sunday mornings and during the week. The kindergarten had given both children a good start. He felt proud that his son had won a scholarship to one of the best secondary schools in Kingston. While his daughter's teacher had told his wife, that she was confident that her daughter would also pass her examinations when she took them.

His decision to go to England and leave his wife with the children had been a good one. He had missed them over the years, but work had filled the lonely hours, and now they were together once again. People had advised him to send for his wife, they could both work and send for the children later when they could afford to. But he had shuddered at the thought of separating them and leaving some behind in Jamaica without their mother. They had always been a close-knit family. His aged mother lived in St Elizabeth where he was born. His wife's mother lived closer, in St Mary. They got very little help from them with the children because they could not help.

He and his wife had looked after the children with a little help from her aunt who lived in Kingston. Often, she had helped them out with the leftover foodstuff she could not sell in Coronation market. He had admired her aunt, who bought and sold food in the market six days a week for years. She had managed through her hard work to support her family, in the countryside and those who came to Kingston seeking work, to improve their lives. She was the hub of her family and community. She was a businesswoman. Everyone asked for her help and advice. She had married and buried many family members because she had wisely joined a 'Lodge', contributing her sixpence a month as insurance against unforeseen events. She was the first person in her neighbourhood to have a television set, and her neighbours gladly paid for the privilege of watching this new-fangled entertainment.

Next, she paid a deposit on a two-bedroomed house in one of the new housing schemes in Kingston. Later, she added a third bedroom. Now, she had a comfortable and respectable home in an up and coming neighbourhood. One day, they would be able to visit when they had saved enough money to go on holiday. They could help her now that she was getting on in age, and was no longer selling in the market. She continued her little business in her yard and outside her gate. His wife's aunt had bought most of the furniture for a reasonable sum, it went towards the family's fare to England. Tomorrow he would take the children to the little school not far from the house. He would ask about work for her. They would also have to find a nanny for the youngest girl who was not at school yet. The island communities, around Herne Hill Road, knew what do and what was available. As the day brightened, the children dressed in their oversized coats and shoes walked beside or behind their parents, something they were enjoying after three long years. They walked down Herne Hill Road, and as they walked towards the big junction their moods began to change, and they became more agitated and fearful.

The houses got smaller and shabbier. There were large scruffy buildings on both sides of the road and railway arches above with rattling trains. By the time, they got to the junction they were terrified.

They saw run-down shops and peeling railway arches holding up the tracks on which trains rumbled. They did not like this end of their road. They were glad they did not live in the rectangular building with many windows, or in any of the buildings at this end of the street. They hoped they would not have to come to this end of the road again.

He pointed to the entrance of the railway station, as well as the bus stop for both the 35 and 45 buses. He told them that the two buses took workers across London, from the crack of dawn to work in the factories, shops and offices. The transport would take them to Brixton to buy food as well. The children were relieved as they walked up the road and back towards their home. Their dream of a good life in England had been shaken by the shabbiness of the junction and the bleak railway arches. They decided that they would only think about the roads near their home and their three-storey house that was big but not shabby.

They entered the playground of St Saviour's school a few yards from their house. Noisily, children played in the playground, they kept close to their parents. Eventually, the head teacher approached and ushered them into his small office. He took their details and informed the parents, that he would gladly take all of them into his tiny school except the two oldest and the youngest.

The parents were relieved that four children were off their hands on a day to day basis. They asked where to get information about the eldest children and were told to go to the Town Hall in Brixton. They left the school building and small playground. The father led them beyond the school. Not far from the school and their house was an unopened gate, it was closed for the day. The young ones screeched, as they saw the endless grassy areas surrounded by what seemed like leafless dead trees. They grabbed hold of the railings and placed their faces between them, to look at the vast play space that awaited them. They pushed the gate to enter, it did not open, it was firmly locked.

"Dem lock it at 4 o'clock in winter," the father told the disappointed children.

Mi wi tek oonu at di weekend and oonu can run and play all oonu want," he informed them.

The parents were happy with the surprise. The kids could use the park in the light summer evenings and on weekends. They had Saturday mornings to explore and use the secret garden until summer arrived. The secret garden made up for their disenchantment with the far end of their road and the small front and backyard. Secretly, they vowed to stay where they lived in the middle of the road.

The secret garden in Ruskin Park.
Photo: B Ellis

St. Saviour's Primary School.
Photo: B Ellis

CHAPTER 7

Settling in

The family stayed together for the rest of the week. They used their mini family holiday to settle in, as well as to learn about their new surroundings. The children needed new clothing and equipment for school the following week. The parents had to find a nanny for the non-school age girl within the community, and secondary schools for the two oldest children. They could not leave them at home, so they trotted everywhere with them in their oversized coats, to the amusement of all those came across them.

The honeymoon was over. The smell of bacon and eggs did not fill the small flat anymore. They ate toast with margarine and black tea with milk for breakfast now. Sometimes, if their mother was not too busy, she made cornmeal porridge flavoured with nutmeg and cinnamon. They remembered the porridge, as back home breakfast and they liked it. The following morning, the youngsters dressed and sauntered towards the dingy end of the street, full of fear. The family stood by the bus stop in front of a couple of ramshackle shops. They could not see inside them, either because they were not tall enough, or because their fronts were covered with paper from the inside.

They waited a few minutes, then two buses came, they were amazed. In Kingston, they had stood at the top of the lane for what seemed like hours, before they could squeeze into one of the small buses that came along. The 'patty pan' the people had affectionately called them. Once they had squeezed into the 'patty pan', they held their breath for the remainder of the journey, it felt as if hundreds of bodies had squeezed into the bus at every stop. Now they had a choice of two big red buses, they boarded the bus with the fewest people, and the adults paid the fares. The conscientious and proud black conductor in his dark blue uniform and cap pressed the cost of the tickets into his silver machine, then reeled off ribbons of paper tickets and playfully handed it to the children. They scrambled for the upper deck but were ordered to sit downstairs. The bus drove along Coldharbour Lane, stopped at the lights, then sped past some big old houses on the right and left of the road, before turning right at the corner into Gresham Road, by a shop selling gardening and hardware tools. Their father pointed out Brixton police station, as the buses dutifully stopped in front of it. He warned them that if they did not behave, the police would know about it.

The 35-bus moved off. Promptly, it stopped at the lights, then turned left along the busy Brixton Road with big and small shops on either side, before it reached the railway bridge across the road. Again, their father pointed out the landmarks; the side streets housed Brixton market. The big post office was across the road, close to the big Bon Marche store; Morley's store was further up the main road. They would visit the market on their way back. The bus continued up the busy main street and drove around St Matthews's Church in the middle of the road. For the first time, they saw lots of black people moving about in the bustling streets. The bus joined the main road again and turned left into Acre Lane, outside a building with a prominent clock. They got off and entered the lobby of the old and drab Town Hall. Inside an assistant came forward and asked if she could help.

Breathlessly, the parents and children trooped up two flights of tiny winding stairs, to the education section on the second floor behind the assistant. They picked up leaflets and looked at them as if they could give them the information, they were seeking. The adults were ushered into a small room, while the first assistant watched over the children. An ageing education officer told the parents that there were a few schools, in the neighbourhood with many immigrant children. A few bus stops, up the road, there was a girl's school, many girls from the 'islands' went there, Parkside Girl's School it was called. The head teacher, Madam West was from Switzerland,

and she was an excellent headteacher. It would be a good school for the girl. The boy was a bit more problematic because there were not many boys' schools, in the area.

However, there was a 'special school' at the top of Brixton Hill, not far from the Town Hall. The children of immigrants went there. The education officer confidently told them that he knew that the boys were getting the best education possible in this school. Proudly, the mother informed the schools' officer that her son had passed the high school exam in Jamaica, and was about to attend one of the best schools in the island's capital. She showed him the letter that confirmed that her son had passed the exam. Curiously, the officer had looked at it and quickly returned it to the proud parents. The couple were satisfied that they had found the right school for their bright, intelligent son, and it was not far from their home, they took the information. The officer said he would contact the schools, to see when the children could be enrolled the following week.

The mother and father were delighted with the morning's outing. They left the building and walked to the traffic lights and crossed the main road, to the shopping district. They were almost directly, in front of Woolworths. They walked into the store with the children, and went to the pick and mix stand and took a bowl, then each child was allowed the joy of choosing a couple of sweets. The youths selected the brightest coloured sweets. They left Woolworths and turned left into Coldharbour Lane, at the top of the market. Their father pointed to the small cinema across the road, many children went there on Saturday mornings, to watch films he told them. The youngsters asked if they could go too, their father promised them he would work something out.

The brood walked along Coldharbour Lane to the junction with Atlantic Avenue and crossed over in front of a butcher's shop on the corner, owned by a Greek family. The butchers welcomed Mr Brown and asked if he had come for his usual order. Mr Brown introduced his over-sized family to them, they greeted the children and his wife and smiled and laughed with them.

"Your husband loves lamb, Mrs Brown," said the senior butcher in his Greek-English accent.

She didn't know how to respond. She smiled and smiled, already she was meeting all shades of 'white people' trying to speak the English language correctly like herself.

"A shoulder of lamb," enquired a younger butcher.

Mr Brown grinned an agreeable 'yes' and added to his usual order.

"Two pounds of lamb neck, two boiling chickens, a dozen eggs, mi wife want a dozen okras, and she will pick out a few scotch bonnet peppa too," he said proudly.

"A haffi feed mi big fambly now," he told the butcher's assistant smiling.

The elderly Greek butcher looked approvingly at his customer and said.

"Yes, we must take care of our families; in my country, the family is everything."

"She a go cum wid one a di big one dem fi buy meat from now on, mi will be working hard fi feed all a dem," the father smiled.

They collected their order, and the mature Greek butcher embraced Mr Brown and waved the family goodbye. They walked to the corner and crossed at the lights again, this time they were in front of one of the stalls at the side of a railway arch, with foodstuff from the islands and the mainland. Mr Brown pointed out the Labour Exchange to his family, below the market's entrance and informed them that was where the workers went to get jobs after they had left the air raid shelters on Clapham Common in 1948.

A white woman spoke to their parents in English and Jamaican. They stared at her and wondered how a white person could talk like them. The parents scrutinised the yams, bunches of green bananas, plantains and sweet potatoes, made their choice and paid for them. As they walked away, a tall black man entered the small enclave at the back of the stall. Hurriedly, Mr Brown introduced his wife and family to him.

"Mi fambly come last Sunday," he said to his fellow countryman.

The man shook the children's hands, smiled and quickly disappeared.

"A fi im food stall, di white ooman look afta it fah im," he informed his wife.

The family strolled through the extensive arcade, towards the far end of Brixton market. A variety of foodstuff and smells from around the world filled the covered marketplace. There were rows and rows of stalls selling household and other goods. The parents stopped in front of a large fish stall on the right. Again, the fishes were scrutinised for the biggest and freshest, and their order was placed. The red snappers were cleaned and sliced and given to the eldest child. Next, to the fish stall was an opening which led to the back of the stalls.

Next, to it was Mr Martlyn's little shop, stuffed with black hair products, carbolic soap, combs and bits and pieces from the islands and the mainland. Again, Mr Brown proudly introduced them to Mr Martlyn. The stallholder was of medium height, a stocky black man who had been one of the first business people in Brixton. The tubby shop owner rubbed their heads and told them to learn at school, and to be kind to their parents. As they walked away, he handed each child a sweet and grinned at them. Soon, Mr Martlyn was in conversations with other customers seeking his wares.

They turned right at the end of the arcade, where there were some fruit and vegetable stalls on one side, and a variety of bric-a-brac stalls on the other. They bought fruit and vegetables, apples, ripe bananas, tangerines, pears, potatoes and cabbage. The father gave each child a fruit as a treat for their long day, finding schools and shopping. They continued along the small street, before turning left into another road with rows and rows of medium-sized shops.

Towards the end of the road, just before Brixton's main street, there were stores within the railway arches. The parents went to the shop that sold ham, sausages and other delicacies. Next door, the smell of baking bread, buns and sweetmeats in Gregg's bakery made the children feel hungry. Quickly, the parents purchased some ham and eggs and left. They walked along Brixton Road towards the bus stop in front of the police station. They waited a few minutes for their transport to take them home, promptly the 35-bus arrived. Their father rang the bell, and the bus dutifully stopped outside the 'bag wash', in Loughborough Junction.

The old railway station's entrance and its worn arches, revived their fearfulness as they walked under them to the traffic lights, to cross and walk to their home. The rumbling trains above amplified their uneasiness about this end of their road. Their father showed them the dentist and doctor's surgeries on the main road. Johnson's button factory clung to the corner of the junction, red brick and plain.

"A lot a ooman from back home wuk dere. Dem seh di pay small, but it near di house, yuh doan haffi tek no bus," he informed his wife.

She agreed with him.

Impatient, to flee the shabby and threatening junction, the youths shuffled towards the middle of their road, looking back to make sure their parents were not too far behind. The family enjoyed their first weekend together in three years. The holiday was over. The start of their new life in Britain was about to begin. They felt happy, even though they did not like this end of their road. Everything, they wanted was in the centre of their road, the church, their school, the park, their parents and the red-bricked Carnegie Library across from their school.

The head teacher had told the family that some classes visited the library each week and that the pupils could borrow up to three books to take home. The location of their home was the best place to be, they felt sorry for anybody that lived below their three-storey flat fronted house and its tiny front garden.

The scary bridge the children walked under.
Photo: B. Ellis

Brixton market's central arcade
Photo: B. Ellis

Lambeth Town Hall, Brixton
Photo: B. Ellis

A conductor under training
Courtesy of London Transport Museum

The meat shop Atlantic Avenue, Brixton.
Photo: B Ellis

CHAPTER 8

Mrs Cann

The children were too insecure to explore beyond their immediate surroundings. The junction terrified them, with the constant rumble of trains on the rattling bridges and peeling shop fronts; the top of the road was too far away to stimulate their curiosity. They were delighted that their home, the secret garden as well as the red-bricked building their father had said was a library, were all within walking distance of their home. The younger children had not understood this piece of information, but the eldest among them had understood it, maybe this would be his secret place to discover. The November evenings were too dark to venture into the park, and the gates would be locked by the time they left school. Nevertheless, they eyed up the entrance as their sister led them the short distance home. Saturday mornings would be light enough, to explore beyond the bolted gates and railings that had kept them out, since their arrival.

One afternoon, as they entered their big house on three floors; they encountered a short, plump woman of about 45 years or so with flaming red hair and the whitest skin. They had not seen her before, and they wondered what she was doing in the house. She stopped and peered at them, and in an accent, they would come to know and understand she asked them how they were.

"You all must be the children of Mr Brown, Mrs Cann told me dat yuh all come last Sunday", she said smiling at them showing her missing and stained white teeth.

She lurked in the hallway, and presently a black man appeared from the middle landing. She introduced him to them as her husband.

He nodded casually at them and entered Mrs Cann's flat. She informed them that he was Mrs Cann's nephew and that they lived together on the middle floor. They shuddered. They were glad that they didn't live in the dimly lit flat next to the toilet. They wondered if the comings and goings in the house did not disturb them. They would hold everything in tightly, so that they would only use the middle floor toilet when they were desperate, and certainly not in the dark and at night. Daily, they played a game of 'pass the middle floor as fast as you can.' They tiptoed downstairs to use the ground floor toilet, whenever they thought Mrs Cann was not looking.

Joan explained to the children that she had been in Ireland, at a family funeral and had just returned to London. Proudly, she explained to them that she had got the flat for Mrs Cann and her family. She told them it was hard to get houses, in London if you were from Ireland, the Caribbean or Africa.

"So wi haffi help each odda," Joan had said striving to impress them with her command of the Jamaican language.

The youngsters were confused. This was the second time, they had met a white woman in their short time in England, attempting to speak like them. She told them that her brother had managed to get the rooms, on the middle floor initially, from the Jewish landlord Mr Divokin who had bought the house, a few years before. He had come over from Ireland, to work on the alterations to the house for the owner. Her brother had invited all his family members, to live and share the building with him when the work was completed. Several family members had also come over from Ireland seeking employment. They were glad to have a place to stay. The house became an 'Irish home.' It was a place where Irish people seeking a home could live and feel comfortable in London. Now, they could look in disgust, at the houses with signs which brazenly said 'No Irish, no Blacks, no dogs. The English people she told the children "Dem hate wi more dan yuh". The children were puzzled.

She told them that she had lived with her daughters, other family members and many, many Irish people in the house. The place was crammed with Irish people she laughed. Many of her family members over the years had managed to get council houses, flats, or bought their own homes, and had given up the top and ground floor apartments. She had begged the Jewish property owner, to let it to Mrs Cann and her family, which he did. Then she explained, that one day their father had come knocking on the door, asking if there were any rooms to rent. Mr Brown had told her that his family was coming from Jamaica very soon, and he needed more rooms to accommodate them. She spoke to the landlord, and because Mrs Cann already had children in the house, he could not refuse. She told him when he returned that he could have the upstairs flat. He had given up his one room in Stockwell and moved to the house to wait for them.

Mrs Cann's nephew came out of the ground floor flat, he turned to Joan and said: "Cum mek wi go dung a di betting shop."

The couple left the house, the children wondered about their strange neighbours.

Mr Brown's routine became the family's routine. By six o'clock each morning, he was on his way to one of his many assignments inside London or in the Home Counties. The bridges of London, the houses and factories needed his skill and attention to detail. Mrs Brown was left with the care of the children and the running of the home, as well as the new job that was awaiting her. She had spent a few weeks finding her way around, settling the children into their new schools all six of them, as well as finding a nanny for the youngest, so she could work.

The ambitious migrants had spread themselves across London and many British towns and cities. The pioneers had been forced to live in the redundant World War II air raid shelters beneath Clapham South when they arrived, as no accommodation had been prepared for them by their reluctant hosts because they were not wanted. After some months, they had spread out from Clapham South into Battersea, Balham, Brixton, Clapham, Streatham, Stockwell, Herne Hill, Brockley, Catford, East Dulwich, Camberwell, Lewisham, North and East London, South-West London and West London.

Wherever, there were factories, schools, crumbling old houses with blighted neighbourhoods they willingly put down roots. They could live in these homes and areas and keep them ticking over until the young white population returned to reclaim them. They had been grudgingly invited for their labour only, most of the British people did not know that they had been asked to come and work. So, they concluded that someone in a government department had come up with this well-crafted scheme to force down white working-class people's wage demands, by importing workers from the colonies. These business people were intent on maintaining their power and profit margins whatever the cost. The first and second world wars 1914-18 and then 1939-45, had taken the lives of thousands of the white male population and caused great hardship and sacrifice for everyone.

White working-class men had fought in the trenches in Europe, The Middle East and Africa alongside the black and brown volunteer soldiers from the islands, the mainland, Africa and Asia. The women had been employed in the hospitals, munitions factories, industry, transport and on farms growing food to support the war effort. Hitler's bomb raids throughout the island had fallen on both the well to do and working people, they had devastated their homes, families, communities and future.

White working-class men had returned from both wars as heroes, they had been promised homes and employment fit for heroes. Now businesses, corporations and governments were using the age-old trump card, divide and rule against all working people. The ruling classes would use the black and Asian poverty-stricken labour force they had created in the colonies, to keep wages low in post-war Britain and wipe out any monetary gains they as working people and war heroes had fought and died for.

It had happened before, the British ruling classes and the plantocracy had used slave labour to build wealth and an empire before 1838. After the enslaved Africans had liberated themselves from slavery, the planters and government refused to pay them a decent wage. Instead, they had brought workers to the plantations from Europe, India, China and other countries to work on the estates. Now, in post-war Britain the bargaining power of white British workers was being undermined by workers, from the empire, it would continue to be the weapon of governments, business and corporations, and the ruling elite in the decades to come.

The ambitious immigrants were eager to transform their social and economic status, in the United Kingdom, and the world. Unskilled work in the cities and towns of the British Isles would provide the opportunities, they had yearned for since their ancestors' liberation. Slavery had fashioned and crafted the African personality to throw off obstacles placed in their way. They would use their organisations and their communities to support themselves, their growing families in this cold and bleak land.

The incoming workers had found it relatively easy to get and change jobs because of the reconstruction efforts and the shortage of white workers. This may have worked in their favour and given them the opportunity to increase their wages by moving from job to job, thus giving them a slight advantage for a while. Mrs Cann worked in the button factory at the bottom of Herne Hill Road, in the brick building that clung to the junction. The company was in constant need of workers because the pay was poor. The white working-class women who wanted to work had shunned these workplaces, because of the low wages, this had made it easy for the incoming workers to get employment quickly. Many local mothers, and especially those from the arriving immigrant communities worked in these factories, for whatever the management paid them. Mrs Cann's energy and drive had made her the women's advisor, big sister and unofficial trade union rep in the workplace as well as in her community. The woman's feistiness would make her the leader of any small group. She duly told the women their rights in the workplace; as well as the duties of the males and females in the home. She informed the women how the bills were shared out between husband and wives, and how to conduct their relationship with their spouses.

She told Mrs Brown about the job at the button factory. She had also informed her, that the supervisor would give her the worst tasks and buttons to sew so she would not be able to get any bonus, at the end of the week. She would have to do a lot of overtime, to make up her wages of five pounds for a forty-hour week, to seven pounds. She also told her that they had recently found out, that the managers were paying the white workers more money for the same job. She informed her that the whites were always given the best buttons and overtime, to make up their wages. She told her to ask for decent buttons so she could make a little money too.

"Dem is de laziest people dat God blow breath eena, ef di lickle sun cum out dem nah cum a wuk, dem gwaan on holiday, dem nah wuk. Mi si dem eena di park a tek sun but dem no like wi because wi black and wi wuk hard, fah di lickle money dem gi wi," she told them.

She pointed out time and time again to the women that she had not come to England, to be white people's slave once more. Her fore parents had done enough of that during slavery. She was going to get every penny she worked for, and she was not going to break her back to get it. In Jamaica, the islands and on the mainland, they had all worked for white people. They got little or nothing for their labour, only the cast offs the families had outgrown. She had fled from Trelawny to Britain to end the humiliation, and she was not going through it again.

She looked at Mrs Brown, and the other women gathered around her and told them. "Dem days dun lang time, wi gwine get all wha wi fi get dis time around."

The women nodded in agreement.

"Slavery dun lang time, wi haffi get wha wi wuk fah fram now on," they all agreed.

Mrs Cann had left the Caribbean to improve herself and her family. She wanted an excellent education for her children and was working and saving for a big enough place for them. The mother needed to earn enough money to look after her parents and children back home. However, she was not going to beg or play the fool, she would get back as much as she put in without the usual loss of face. The husbands and managers in the workplace were terrified of her 'mouth.' They told their wives and the workers not to listen to this loud-mouthed woman, who didn't know anything anyway.

Carnegie Library - Herne Hill Road

Photo: B. Ellis

CHAPTER 9

Mrs Brown

Her daughter's nanny had decided to join her relatives in America. When Mrs Brown collected the child after work, from across the road, the childminder had told her that she was looking forward to going to live in America.

"Americans were not as racist as the British." she had said. "If you work hard you would get on and make something of yourself there, but here in Britain it was not possible, even if a person worked every day of the week, they still wouldn't get anywhere."

Mrs Phillips had been in the country ten years, she had arrived sometime after the Windrush, and had left her young son back home with her mother in Antigua, she had sent for him as soon as she could. When he arrived, she realised it was not going to be easy, children needed stability, it was not easy to live in a room in someone's house or move about because of the child's schooling. Dutifully, she had thrown her pardner each week and saved as much as she could from her small wage, she did all the overtime that was available.

When she got her 'pardner draw', she had searched for a little house or flat to buy for herself and her child. She had found a house on the corner of Herne Hill and Alderton Road, most of the rooms were small, but she could rent out some of them to help pay the mortgage. Initially, she had come for five years only and had hoped to return home, to live with her young son. She had worked hard and turned her hand to all sorts of things, to make a little money to be comfortable. But, she had found that however hard she worked, she was not promoted, so her wages remained the same. She was paying for her little house as well as paying the regular and the unexpected bills. And even with lodgers and a husband now, she was still struggling to make ends meet, and life didn't seem to be getting better for her and her small family.

So, her family had told her to come to America, they were doing ok, and she would too, she was leaving in two months' time. It had been convenient for Mrs Brown because her house was opposite the flat. The mother could look out of her window in the mornings, and see the comings and goings in Mrs Phillips' house as her lodgers left for work. Sometimes, when she was doing overtime at the button factory, one of the older children was sent to collect the child. The arrangement was very advantageous to her, she would miss her, she would have to find someone else to look after the girl, so she could continue to work.

The children had settled into their new schools and country well, the nearby school and its classrooms were small with a stable staff, who were dedicated to the pupil's learning and welfare. This helped the mother to feel secure that they were in good hands while she was working. The youngsters loved their new school, and were head-over-heels with the secret garden, they were saints at school and even better at home, their reward would be the secret garden at the end of the week. Promptly, they carried out their little chores and homework, to free up Saturday mornings to fulfil their desires.

Soon, they were exploring more than the secret garden, school friends had invited them to the kids' film club at the local cinema in Brixton, on Saturday mornings. The eldest boy had the invitation. However, all of them wanted to go too, he moaned, and moaned but took them anyway because he did not want to miss the opportunity. Nervously, the kids walked behind their brother as they prepared to walk to the feared junction. The youngsters did not want to go that way, but it was the only way to the 35-bus stop that would take them to Brixton and the cinema. They wished they could fly to the end of the road. Quietly, they closed the front door and walked out into the small front garden guardedly, and then onto Herne Hill Road timidly. The youths had never made this journey before without one of their parents; they sauntered along the solid pavement scanning the path ahead for any danger.

Suddenly, they heard the distant rumbling of a train approaching the station, the rattle of the train on the peeling bridges above, terrified them. They froze and waited patiently for the train to pass, they didn't want it to fall on them. Their older brother laughed at them and called them scaredy-cats. As they scrambled onto the bus, their fears subsided, and their sense of adventure returned, they squabbled about the curling paper tickets from the efficient black conductor's shiny machine. The children watched cartoons for the first time and could not wait to share this magical experience with their parents on returning home.

Luckily, for Mrs Brown, there was a local Boy's Brigade group at a nearby church hall. Mr Hewitt, the Brigade's leader, was always recruiting for his troupe. He found it easier to sign up youngsters from the newly arrived immigrant communities, because almost all the parents were churchgoers, and they knew more about the teachings of the Bible than the local white population. The newcomers were regular and devoted churchgoers, and his church welcomed them, although he knew that many of the local white churches were reluctant to open their doors to immigrants from the Caribbean and Africa. Many of these churches and congregations made them feel very unwelcome.

So, the new arrivals well-versed in the Bible and the Lord's teachings had set up their own churches, in whatever improvised buildings they could find. They did not mind too much being rejected by their hosts because the churches they had visited were uninviting, cold, drab and stiff like the host community. They preferred the swaying and moving sermons, of their churches back home. The Windrush and subsequent ships had brought many preachers and pastors in waiting, from back home to recruit members for their places of worship, to thank and praise the creator, that had helped them so far, in their quest to improve their lives.

Mr Hewitt had signed up their sons for his pack, giving the newly arrived parents a much-needed break, some evenings and sometimes at the weekend. This gave the boys direction and continuity, and they were kept busy during the school holiday with activities. The youths and some of the younger children, were extremely fortunate because they had supervised activities outside the family on a regular basis, this helped them to settle into the host community. Their extended families were thousands of miles away in the islands, they were alone in a foreign land, and so they bonded to keep out the hostility around them. The youngest children had settled and were enjoying their new school. However, one of the girls was frightened of one of her teachers. Every Thursday morning, she cried to Mrs Brown:

"Mrs Millwall is coming today; I don't want to go to school."

The mother had asked the child repeatedly why she was afraid of the teacher, the child only stuttered and looked fearful and repeated her wailing, Mrs Millwall is coming today. She had gone to the school and had spoken to the head teacher during her lunch break from the button factory. Mr Grubb, the head teacher, had welcomed her and listened to her concerns. He explained that the pupils felt that Mrs Millwall was very strict, she had high aspirations for all the children and expected all her pupils to tell her what she had taught them the previous week. Some new children found this upsetting, and there were many similar complaints from parents about their children not wanting to come to school. He then arranged a meeting with the mother, teacher and child to sort out the matter. The girl had understood the teacher, but the parent's troubles were just about to begin.

Then her eldest son began to complain about his school too. The youngsters always came to her with their problems; they never went to their father. He was busy working all the hours that God sent. She listened to her son's complaints. She would go to his school as she had done with her daughter and talk to the head teacher and teacher. Her son told her that the work was too easy for him, he finished his work after a few minutes and stared out of the window. His teachers said he was rude and disrespectful because of this, but he did not know what to do after he finished.

He begged to go back to school in Jamaica because the teachers there gave the students hard work, and he preferred this. The other students from the islands and the mainland also did not like the school. It was not like schools back home where you had to do a lot of work, and the teachers expected you to work hard every minute of the day, and pass difficult exams at the end of the term and school year. The boys knew that their parents had brought them to England, to do hard work and pass exams to get good jobs. They did not want to let their parents down, they wanted them to be proud of them, they knew how hard their parents worked to send them to school each day.

These pupils did not want to stay at this school because the white children did easy work. The students from the islands including himself did not play with them because they were not easy to play with, so they were punished. He did not want to go to school. He begged her to find him another school. She listened but told him he had to stay for the foreseeable future. She took a week off 'sick' from the button factory. If any of her fellow workers saw her, she would say she was going to the doctor. She changed buses in Brixton and went to the head teacher's office. The headteacher welcomed her and told her he was glad to see her. He informed her that her son was withdrawn and sulky at times. He had not settled into the school community, and he was not getting on with the other students and his teachers. The boy was refusing to do the class work because he said it was too easy, the teacher had given him extended activities, but he still complained. He had to think about the well-being of all the school community. He had made him stay in during breaks, but this had not changed his behaviour. He was upsetting the smooth running of his school and students.

He told Mrs Brown that his major concern was that her son was a born leader, and his classmates from the islands, the mainland and some of the white pupils, hung on to his every word and actions. He had been seriously thinking of excluding him for a week or so, to see if he would mend his ways. This would allow the other students to settle down, and get back into the schools' routine. She begged him not to exclude her son. She told him that in Jamaica she had no problem with him, he was engrossed in his lessons and did his homework. Her son was bright and had done well at school in Jamaica and had won a scholarship to one of the best schools on the island. She had joined her husband in England because they felt that all their children would have a better chance of getting the best possible education here. She told the head teacher that she would talk to her son, and ask him to cooperate with his teachers.

The family were distressed about the visit to the school. The children begged their brother, to do as he was told so that he would not be excluded from school because they loved him dearly. The parents lectured their children about their behaviour in their schools. They were told to try and speak the way the white children spoke, in their classrooms because that was the proper way to speak English. They should try to learn everything they could about England because the family were now living in London, later, they could learn about Jamaica and the islands and talk in Jamaican. They were told that if they spoke English correctly, they would go to university, get well-paid jobs and live in lovely houses. They could buy one of those big houses at the top of their road in Denmark Hill. They would have everything their parents did not have. In the meantime, she had to find him another school.

The family did not know it then, that the community and their children would have to collectively take on the British education system, to get the schooling they wanted for their offsprings. In the islands and the mainland, children went to school to learn, and the parents could trust the school and teacher to make sure the children worked to the best of their ability. The parents remembered their schooling in the makeshift classrooms with many, many pupils, the teachers and their thick straps that made them learn. They thought it would be the same in their adopted country, that their children's schools would make them learn. There were schools on every street corner, almost as many as public houses, their children would do well in this well-resourced country, they had assumed.

However, many immigrant parents would eventually learn, that schools in Britain did not think highly of their own white working-class students, their parents and their communities. They saw these communities as problematic. These parents did not know at their arrival, that the British school system was not built on the principle that all pupils were competent learners with the ability to succeed. The schools and educational institutions in their adopted country were tripartite, they catered for three distinct ability groups separately.

Historically, the British School system had evolved to cater for three types of pupils, those with learning disabilities, the average child and the very able to be taught in different schools. The run-down schools in their communities operated on these principles. Their children would be viewed by the British education system and many teachers as 'problems' because they had come from the islands and the mainland, they were black and working-class and because they lived in the decaying inner cities. Continuously, the invited workers would have to take on the education system in the decades to come, to make it work for them and their children.

The British school system at the time was under pressure, white, black and Asian parents were making demands on the schools and the education system, to respond to their children's natural educational abilities and aspirations. White working-class parents did not want their children in the same classrooms with pupils from India and Pakistan. They said that these pupils would hold back their children's learning as well as students from the islands and the mainland who did not speak English properly and were not up to the standard of their mainstream white classmates.

Solutions had to be found, white parents had to be appeased, many local education authorities took the predictable path, small groups of Indian and Pakistani children were driven in buses from their communities to all white schools miles away. The education authorities had justified this policy, by saying it would help the non-English speaking children learn English quickly, from their white English-speaking peers, as well as integrating them into the majority culture. The result of bussing pupils out of their communities, limited the numbers of non-speakers of English, in any one class, school or catchment area in the Local Education Authorities.

Considerable cohorts of young boys arriving from the islands and the mainland were sent to schools, which catered for pupils with learning and physical disabilities. Some of the arriving children were assessed on diagnostic tests that were unfamiliar to them because they did not know the society or context. Many of them did poorly on these tests and were allocated to the nearest schools, and some were not tested at all. A significant number of students were sent to schools for the educationally sub-normal. In 1971, Bernard Coard, summed up the concerns of the community and parents in the pamphlet 'How the West Indian Child is made Educationally Sub Normal in the British School System', published by New Beacon Books in 1971. He had taught in two ESN schools in East London.

The booklet became the focus for the black Education, the black Parents and Supplementaty Schools' Movements, as well as community activists throughout the United Kingdom. The Caribbean Education and Community Workers' Association (CECWA) was a group of West Indian teachers, social workers, educational psychologists and community workers who campaigned to improve conditions for the Caribbean community in Britain. New Beacon and Bogle L'Ouverture books played an instrumental role in the campaigns, both in organising events and in publicising the movement's work. In the early days, Bogle L'Overture also published the poetry of Linton Kwesi Johnson, Valerie Bloom and the writings of Walter Rodney the Guyanese historian. From the very beginning, members of the George Padmore Institute have recorded and led the struggle of the community for education and continues to campaign and support the demand for the British education system to provide equality of access and outcomes in education for all pupils.

Bernard and Phyllis Coard, Maureen Stone, Darcus Howe, Olive Morris, Jessica Huntley, Farrukh Dhondy, John La Rose, Roxy Harris, Gus John, Ansel Wong, parents and many committed community members, supported the campaigns. They challenged and explained to the arriving communities, the education authorities' policies, practices and the consequences for their children. The black Supplementary Schools' movement took responsibility on Saturday mornings, in the island and the mainland communities in the inner cities of the United Kingdom, to do the job the British school system seemed incapable of doing for the children, from the islands and those born in Britain.

The first recorded Supplementary school was set up in 1967, in Handsworth Birmingham, by Bini Brown, community members and parents. Two years later in 1969, the George Padmore and the Albertina Sylvester Supplementary Schools were set up by John La Rose and parents in North London. The George Padmore school catered for pupils in secondary schools, while the Albertina Sylvester school taught the primary age range.

Mrs Brown and her son were caught up in the British school system's assumptions, and practices, about learning and the type of pupils that could learn and benefit from academic education. She was reluctant to discuss her problems with her work colleagues because she did not want anyone to know, that her eldest child was said to be disruptive in school. She remembered that she may have told one of her workmates, that her son had passed the high school examination in Jamaica, but now the school was saying he was disruptive and not learning at all. The island and mainland parents had high hopes and expectations for their children's future, they wanted their children to do better than they had done and were doing. Willingly, they had come to work in unskilled jobs, with low pay and had taken abuse daily from their fellow white workers and managers. They wanted to earn enough money to keep their children in school, at the highest levels and return home after five years. Daily, these goals were slipping away from them.

Peeling shopfront in Coldharbour Lane
Photo: B. Ellis

CHAPTER 10

The women's place

That Saturday afternoon, as she knocked on the door of one of the small row of the picture painted houses in Poplar Road, not far from Herne Hill Road where she lived; the mother felt she was carrying an overwhelming weight on her shoulders. A slim, medium height woman opened the door. She was much older than Mrs Brown, with a light brown complexion. She must have been stunning in her youth, back home, they would call her a 'brown woman' with all the status this implied. Her hairdressing parlour within had reinstated the standing, she had lost when she had migrated to Britain with her husband seeking a brighter future. To the white population, she was just another island woman doing menial work.

Auntie Mackie had somehow managed to get one of the small picture painted terraced houses, from the local council. They were squashed and shabby on the outside, without fences to hide their non-existent scruffy front gardens if space had been made for them. The terraces opened onto the pavement displaying their squashed interiors. They propped each other up in a row of crumbling dwellings. In this row of houses, the women found their breathing space. They accommodated the islands and the mainland's ambitious and aspiring female migrants. They stood in a road that twisted its way, towards the bottom of the shabby junction with its noisy railway arches, bridges and chugging trains.

Mrs Brown and the hairdresser walked through the narrow passageway, passing the creaking stairs that led upstairs to the sleeping accommodation. They entered the squashed back room, already overflowing with women with their hair in various stages of being attended to. The smell of strongly perfumed hair products lingered. They entered. The mother felt her needs and desires reflected in the seated women. They were away from their families, and they felt relieved and guilty at the same time. They would not own up to these feelings. They were waiting or had already experienced Auntie Mackie's nimble fingers, massaging and caressing away the stress, worries and anxieties between her reassuring island chit-chat, punctuated with the crudest Jamaican swear words.

Momentarily, the women's spirits were renewed, and it restored their belief that they were still attractive women in their prime. Eagerly, they waited for her prized gift, clean, massaged scalps with stylish top-knots to give them back their youthfulness. Temporarily, and only for a limited time, Aunty Mackie's slender, nimble and delicate fingers massaged away the strains and stresses of bringing up young families in the United Kingdom. A tall, broad-shouldered black woman was counting out money and handing it over to one of the women. She reminded Mrs Brown of her grandmother.

Auntie Mackie addressed Mrs Brown, but kept her hands on the grateful recipient's head, while thinking about how much money she would make at the end of the day. She worked weekdays cleaning various institutions for what she described as a pittance. The wages paid the bills. She had gone to one of the leading hairdressing schools in Jamaica, Madam Leon's hairdressing school, now her small house gave her the satisfaction of putting her training into practice and doing what she loved most making women feel young again.

"Aunty Bibs a go start a 'pardna' nex week, she waan more people fi t'row a han or two, yuh waan to," she said without looking at Mrs Brown.

The offer excited the mother, her mind raced. Maybe, the family could begin to think about getting a little house like Mrs Phillips, who was probably settling in her big-lawned home in the United States of America. Mrs Brown said she would, and asked for more details.

She had put a few shillings by when she was in Kingston for a rainy day, here she would do the same. She had to look beyond the small flat they lived in now. This was part of the family's problem, many bodies squeezed into this tiny but cheerful apartment at the top of the three-floor house. There must be a solution. She agreed to throw not one but two hands, of the 'pardna' but did not tell her husband.

The women's conversations in the salon meandered and changed, they talked about all the things that had dampened their spirits and dragged them down, during their hectic week at the top of their voices. They were letting off steam. Aunty Mackie's squashed house in the row of houses had become the 'Women's Place'. It was their sanctuary away from their responsibilities as daughters, mothers, wives and breadwinners. In her hair salon, in the row of houses, their massaged heads and hairstyles revived and restored their confidence. Now, they felt they were more than wives, mothers and daughters in this cold and frosty country, even if it was a fleeting sensation that would not last.

The women were there for each other and the roles allocated to them, now. It became the place where their never-ending worries were voiced, echoed and chewed on as they sought answers to them. They complained about the little money they got each week, from their husbands or the men in their lives. They always worried about how to spend these small amounts to give themselves and their children all the things they needed. Officially, these women were not the 'breadwinners'. However, daily they were preoccupied with how to stretch their money and the 'small contributions' they received from the 'breadwinners' each week, to cover the endless expenses they had, or could not have imagined before their migration.

The men had the standing in Britain and the society they had left behind, but it was the women who did the worrying and expanding of the family's skimpy incomes. Their conversations started, finished and were restarted again and again as the women aired the overlooked parts of their lives; along with the daily demands that gradually took away their youth and vitality. Suddenly, without meaning to, Mrs Brown asked the women if they knew of any good boy's school nearby. She explained proudly that her son had passed his exams in Jamaica, and had won a scholarship to St Georges boy's school. One of the women shrieked.

"An yuh bring im yah," said the woman from under a big white towel wrapped around her head.

"Ef fi mi pickney did pass exams like dat in a Jamaica mi wooda lef him deh. Mi wouldn't bring im yah", she said firmly.

The exchange gave free rein to the women's feelings on the subject. It was as if a door had unexpectedly been flung open, and gave them permission to enter and unburden themselves of one of the critical issues; that had made them make the second leg of the triangular journey, from the islands and the mainland to Britain. One of their sacred migration goals was being violated. Their children's education was their priority, even if the host community and the schools did not know this yet or did not care.

"Mi did tink wen mi eena Jamaica dat di education better yah. Now mi deh yah, mi a fine dat a lot a wi pickney dem hab a lot a problems eena di schools dem," added another mother gloomily.

"Mi did expect more fram di schools dem, dem nuh good fah wi pickney dem a tall," a mother lamented.

"Wi did all believe dat wi pickney dem wooda return home with a good education an run di country, but look wha wi pickney dem a go thru in a dis system, dem nah educate dem a tall," another mother declared.

"Mi go evening classes after wuk fi help mi daughter an mi son, wid dem home wuk because di wuk yah nuh good as back home. Ebery ting different, di way dem dweet an di pickney dem confuse. Wi haffi help dem a lot, di schools dem doan care bout dem education," the woman told them.

"Mi, a look fah a different school fah mi son, oonu know any good ones near Herne Hill Road," asked Mrs Brown.

Instantly, she was answered.

"Dem hab one a Kennington, but im haffi tek a test before dem tek im in, like di examinations back home."

"Mi doan mind dat," she said relieved. "Mi sure him can pass any exam dem gi im".

"Yuh haffi tek him deh. Dem gwine gi im a test an ef im do well den dem tek im."

The women returned to their own private thoughts that they were not going to share, in the 'Women's Place' today. Mrs Brown had one day of her 'sick holiday' left, she would take him to the school in Kennington and ask them to give him a test. Then she would know what to do. They were outside the school before it opened on the first morning of the school week, the mother had not made an appointment. Nevertheless, she was willing to stay there all day until her son's schooling was sorted out.

The secretary told her that the school was full, and they were not taking pupils now. She felt desperate. Before long, a tall, thin white man walked along the corridor towards them and looked into the mother's pleading face. He had seen that look before, so he called her into his office. The assistant hurried in and explained that she had told her that the school could not take new pupils now. Her boss assured her it was ok and asked her to leave.

Hastily, the mother explained the problem, so that the head teacher would understand the situation, he looked at his potential student as the mother talked. Proudly, she told him that her son had passed the high school examination in Jamaica, and would have gone to one of the best secondary schools in Kingston. He was now going to a school in Brixton, and he did not like it. He was always in trouble. She assured the head teacher that her son was a good boy. He was well behaved at home and helped her with the younger children. He went to Carnegie Library across the road after school to read books, and when he was not at the library, he was helping her. He helped his youngster siblings to read and do their homework. The headteacher looked from the desperate mother to the eager and expectant pupil.

He told her he could not promise anything at the moment, it was up to her son. He asked the boy to write about his trip from Jamaica to England. The result might enable him to persuade Mr Singh to have another pupil in his overflowing classroom. The boy began to write about his journey on the ship. It was the worst hour of her life. She watched the pen in his left-hand move across the page, swiftly and confidently back and forth line after line. His slanted handwriting soon filled not one but two pages, four sides. The mother prayed that her son's account of the journey, would please the head teacher and that it would have the correct spelling and words, that would make him accept her child into his school. The head teacher had watched the boy keenly, to see if he would fit into the school. He took the two sheets of paper and told him to go and play. He evaluated the contents.

"You came to England on a ship with seven children, that must have been hard for you," he said to the fretful parent. Cheerfully, he continued, "it seemed that it was an exciting journey for your son and his siblings."

"I have here a graphic description of your three-week journey on board the HMS Ascania. I am experiencing everything that happened on the voyage Mrs Brown. I wish I had been on the ship with you and your family. I'm fascinated by those huge waves that kept the children below deck for days, and the smell of boiling cabbage that always filled the dining room and the ship's cabins. Reassuringly, he smiled at her and said, "you were right to be concerned about your son, you are an excellent parent. I'm sure I will have no problem persuading Mr Singh to have him in his overflowing classroom."

She burst into tears of joy as the head teacher confirmed her son's ability, and a place in Kennington Boy's School. She was glad she had taken her son's complaints seriously about his school. She was fortunate to find a head teacher that had listened to her, and who had given her son a chance to prove himself, by writing about a subject that he had experienced and could relate to. The topic had given the boy the opportunity to show what he could do. The parent and child walked home in calm deliberation, before long the mother spoke to her son to make sure he knew how pleased she was.

"Yuh know she said, Mi haffi buy yuh new uniform fah dis school, I know yuh will wuk hard an pass all yuh exams when di time cum like yuh did in Jamaica."

The mother and her son's broad grins told the family what they had wanted to hear.

"Yuh nuh haffi cook tonight mi wi go an buy fish and chips, mi sure di pickney dem wi like it. An fah yuh mi boy its fish an chips and a patty every Friday evening, ef yuh learn yuh lesson dat di teachers gwine gi yuh," said the father smiling from ear to ear.

Mr Brown saw that his efforts over the years were slowly being fulfilled, he wanted the best education for all his children. He had had to leave school when he was very young, in those days children worked from the age of six, as they had done during slavery. He had to help his mother around the house, as well as helping her dig and plant crops on the plot of ground she worked to grow food to feed them and sell the remainder to buy the little things she could not produce. There was nothing left to send him to the small school over the hill in Newmarket. He would also have to make sure his eldest daughter did as well as his son in school. He had high aspirations for his daughters too. He would buy her a typewriter as soon as he saved some money, then she would not have to work long hours in noisy factories, canteens, shops or on the buses. The young people must do better than their parents, that's why they had brought them to England.

A month had passed before Mrs Brown had enough money to visit Aunty Mackie's energising hair salon again. Her beaming smile told the women the good news. Her son had made it, he had changed schools because he had the ability. The women talked about their experiences of their own schooling back home. They recalled those distant school days that they now longed for, with those passionate and concerned teachers who had worked hard to put skills and knowledge, into their rebellious heads. Now as adults, they fully appreciated what those committed teachers had tried their hardest to give them. At this point in time, they would welcome what had seemed like the harsh attention of those teachers then. Now, they knew that those fierce matrons and masters had cared deeply about them and their futures. Their children's brief experience of the British school system had left them longing for those caring and dedicated individuals for their children. They were rapidly learning, that they had no allies in the institutions that schooled their children in Britain.

At home, in the small districts the teachers, parents and carers had been partners in the schooling and upbringing of the children. Pupils went to school to learn, and if they were not learning, they had to say why. The teachers were always right. The pupils had to adhere to and bend to the school's requirements. If they did not, the parents were duly informed. The local community also reinforced the values of the school and the home. Instinctively, the pupils knew and accepted the results, they worked and achieved to the best of their ability. Others excelled in their classrooms and went on to higher education.

The partnership in the islands and the mainland had produced pupils that were diligent and studious. They all had relatives whose children had done well in school, and this was down to the diligence of their teachers and the parents' supporting them. The innermost desires of these island educators were to see all the children, in their classrooms achieve the tremendous ability and possibilities they knew they had. They had learnt during their teaching careers, that all their pupils performed at different levels, and therefore, their task as educators were to skilfully pull out of the children, the abilities they did not know they had.

From the 1950s, parents had embraced Britain and its school system, to achieve their migration goals for their children. There were primary schools everywhere. In the islands, they could not have imagined so many schools for their primary aged children. However, now they realised that these schools seemed unable or unwilling, to deliver what they had made the ultimate sacrifice for, the education of their children to reach their full potential and to progress naturally in all professions in the United Kingdom. Quickly, they began to realise that they had not fully understood the society that they had migrated to, and were now living and working in. It had invited citizens from its colonies to work in the factories, hospitals and railways because they could not get enough white workers. They were paying them less than their fellow white workers, and they had not provided housing for them or the barest necessities. Therefore, it was not surprising that the same system had no expectation for their children to succeed, and gain social mobility via the school system.

The society and schools expected their children to follow in their footsteps, they were preparing them for manual work only. These parents' concerns and doubts about the British school system's inability to educate their children at this early stage, would prove to be prophetic. The impact of the education system on their children would be borne out in the following decades, as the mountains and mountains of research, reports, government enquiries and targeted funding, concluded that many pupils from the islands and the mainland communities were under attaining in the school system. Hence the explosion of black supplementary schools and the Black Education Movement across the United Kingdom to the present day.

More than four hundred years before, their ancestors had laboured relentlessly on the estates and plantations, to provide the income to finance the planters' lavish lifestyles in the United Kingdom and the colonies. The enslaved people were not paid, no schooling was provided for them. They were forbidden to learn to read and write. Secretly, some of them had taught themselves to read and write to avoid being beaten and punished. History was repeating itself, but in a different setting, in the industrial heartland of Britain from 1948 onwards.

CHAPTER 11

The tea factory – Shoreditch

His enormous and extended beer belly heaved and fell as his blotched red face reddened with rage.

"Keep the b----- production line going, you black b......d. What do you think we pay you for? The b----- production line has never stopped since I have been managing the night shift in this factory. It must only stop at six o'clock tomorrow morning, or else heads will roll," he promised.

The manager straightened his white overalls and returned to the glass office above the production line. She hurried along the line trying to keep the machines carrying the crushed tea leaves moving. She chivvied up the women and told them not to let it stop. If it halted, they would be on their hands and knees picking up tea leaves. Imported tea leaves from India, Sri Lanka and Kenya that should be falling into multi-coloured boxes and sealed for re-export. She half walked, and half ran to the canteen to haul that fat so and so Richard, the engineer onto the factory floor to fix the problem machine, so that the line would not stop. She had had to learn how to keep the machines running and manage the women's output all at the same time. On a good night, her line would be able to exceed their target number of sealed boxes guaranteeing a little bonus for everyone, that was one of her priorities.

Richard was the worst engineer in the tea factory. He was allocated to her the minute she became the production line's supervisor. After setting up the machines for the start of the night shift, he disappeared into the bowels of the grimy Victorian building. The white supervisors did not have this problem, their engineers worked alongside them ensuring that their machines did not stop to get decent bonuses, to boost their skimpy basic salary at the end of the week. She knew she had to deal with the engineer now to keep her job. However, she did not know how. Nightly, the management of the tea factory had sat in the glass-fronted office above the production floor. Like vultures, their eagle eyes skimmed and scanned the production lines for signs of hazards that might halt production. Yet, they had not dealt with the obstruction, they had passed it on to her. She had managed to get him to the production floor by shouting some carefully chosen obscenities at him, as she entered the canteen. He grinned at her, while his eyes wandered across her front and rested on her breasts. He strolled out of the restaurant back to the production area, and serviced the machines and disappeared yet again. She watched him, anger and frustration welled up inside her, she would have to sort him out somehow, and very soon.

The early morning sun's rays hit the dirty grey factory walls signalling dawn. Instantaneously, the tired limbs of the women relaxed and gave way to spells of nodding, indicating night was upon them and they needed to sleep. Hastily, the exhausted night shift workers fled the bleak and dusty factory insides and prepared mentally for their next job, before they could have their night's rest.

Faithfully, the number 35 bus was waiting for them outside Shoreditch Church. The bus route ensured a smooth and rapid transition from the tea factory, for some of the women to their small homes some distance away. The bus stopped outside the row of shabby and dilapidated shops in Coldharbour Lane. Furtively, one of the Irish chargehands poked a bit of paper into her hand. The mother walked briskly up the scruffy end of the road, past the crowd of railway arches as well as the bridges holding up the crisscrossing train lines speeding into the city. She heard her eldest son washing the youngest children as she entered the building. She would not disturb them.

Silently, she crept up the stairs and entered her little home. The supervisor flung off her shoes and coat and went into the kitchen. Her daughter was already preparing breakfast for her host of children and getting them ready for school. Her husband had already left for his assignment somewhere in South East England. She had no-one to talk to about the night's events. The boulder rested on her as she helped to prepare the children for school until sleep finally eradicated it. She slept soundly for a couple of hours. Unfortunately, the night's events would not leave her, and she drifted in and out of sleep. She forced herself to wake up as the nightmare engulfed her, but she could not. She had entered the factory canteen yet again, to ask Richard to do the job they were all being paid a paltry wage to do. He had sneered at her and this time had walked around her, his eyes lingering on her breasts. She had asked him for the second time to return to the factory floor to service the production line machines, and he had shrugged her off and sauntered off in the opposite direction.

She had grabbed hold of his white overalls and had shaken the two hundred and fifty pounds of wobbling white flesh. He had looked startled, and this urged her on. She had shoved him with all her strength, and he had landed on a table. She was empowered by the ease with which she had floored this man twice her size. She had let go of his white overalls, and both of her hands were at his throat. She heard herself shouting "I'm going to kill you if you do not come and fix the b----- machine right now."

She woke from the terrible scene and looked into the frightened eyes of her children. They were upset by their mother's rage. She assured them she was having a nightmare because of a horrible engineer at work. They accepted her explanation and went into their room to put on their house clothes. She prepared a snack and tea for them to soothe away their worry and unspoken fears. Automatically, she made the family's evening meal. She remembered the piece of paper that was stuffed into her hand. She wiped her messy hands and rummaged in her coat pocket for it in the hallway. The note said, 'meet me in the pub at the crossroads of Hinton Road and Loughborough Junction at 8'oclock'. She put it back in her pocket and finished the family's meal. She left the house at 7.45 after recounting the problem to her husband, that he had heard so many times before. She had shown him the crumpled piece of paper and its contents.

A medium height white woman with shoulder-length dark red hair was sitting on a stool near the pub's door. Audrey welcomed her in her broad Irish accent. The occupants of the bar glared at her as she entered, expecting her to turn around and leave their private white space. Their enclave was penetrated not by a black man, but by a black woman, they were outraged.

Audrey came forward and ushered her into a corner so they could talk. She heard the conversation behind her 'a monkey in our pub, why don't they go back to their trees'. They had to ignore it. They did not have time, in less than two hours they would have to be on the factory floor to do the night shift. Audrey ordered a soft drink for her and got straight to the point.

"Mrs Brown, all the managers know that Richard is a b------d. We have all complained about him and refused to work with him. Many a supervisor have left because of him, they are trying you out. They are waiting for you to do something about Richard. If you do not do something, Richard will push you until you are forced to leave. The managers will not intervene, they believe a good supervisor should be able to deal with every situation. It's up to you Mrs Brown, to deal with Richard," she said anxiously.

"Do not tell a soul that we met or what we talked about," she advised.

They finished their drink, Mrs Brown left the pub and waited for the number 35 bus across the road. As she was getting on the bus, she saw Audrey walking towards the bus stop she had just left. That night she waited for the shift to start. As usual, the engineer proceeded in the opposite direction as soon as he had set up the machines, and the production line was running. Mrs Brown made sure the line was flowing smoothly, she steeled herself and strode to the canteen. Richard was enjoying a cup of tea and a cigarette. Calmly, she walked up to him and told him he had a choice. He could return to the line and supervise the machines like all the engineers in the factory, or she would go into the office and make a formal complaint to the managers. She pointed out to him that she did not have to provide any evidence as the bosses' offices, was above the production space. The women and the rest of the factory would back her up. The choice was his, he could return to the production line now or face the consequences.

He ignored her comments and said.

"Mrs Brown, I love those breasts."

The line supervisor left the canteen and waited for a few minutes for his return, then went to the manager's office in the glass dome above the factory floor. She was a little unsteady on her feet and asked for a complaints' form. The managers looked at her and then at each other. Shakily, she took the form and wrote her complaint, she worried that her spelling and handwriting was not what she would like it to be. She had not done well at school, daily she told her children stories about her school days, her difficulties and achievements with her teachers and fellow pupils.

The mother was adamant that her children would be good readers and writers. She had sent them from the age of three to Mrs Scott's kindergarten, near their home in Kingston at a cost, but it was worth it, her children had had a positive attitude to their school work back home and now in this country. Her children would be more than a night supervisor in a tea factory in Shoreditch.

Defiantly, she told them "I'm not a black b------d; I am a black woman and the line's supervisor."

The line supervisor returned to the factory floor, she smoothed out the glitches in the production line that night, she never saw Richard again.

The Tea Factory, Shoreditch
Photo: B. Ellis

CHAPTER 12

A solution

The night shift workers were ecstatic after the disappearance of Richard. They had been sacrificing their nights' sleep and ordinary family life, to ensure that their children were looked after twenty-four hours a day. Richard and the management team had denied them and their families, the rewards of their sacrifice. The engineer and the organisation's negligence, on the factory floor, had made it impossible for the women to earn enough bonus to increase their small wages. The new situation gave the women pride in their work and unity of purpose. Their solidarity and work ethic improved their take-home pay, beyond anything seen in the factory before. The women could now pace themselves throughout the night, and work steadily without the frenzy of the production line stops and starts. They appreciated the line supervisor's efforts. Nightly, they thanked her for her supportive and caring management style, that gave them increases in their pay packets, that made them smile at the end of the week. There was nothing, this group of women would not do for their supervisor and each other. Every new worker, joining the production line knew instinctively what they had to do, they knew each other's circumstances in every respect, and worked cooperatively to improve all their lives. The female night workers covered each other's backs.

However, they could not control the grime and tea dust from the factory floor, entering their outer and inner selves. So, they used a small portion of their end of the month bonus to scrub away the tea dust, that had crept into the cracks and crevasses of their bodies. The women cherished each other, they had shared aspirations.

The following Saturday morning, Mrs Brown strolled to the row of picture painted houses in Poplar Road. Smiling, Auntie Mackie opened the door while shouting orders, to someone in her crudest Jamaican English. When she had finished, she greeted and invited her into her overflowing hair salon.

"Cum, cum nuh, sit dung mi hab nuff heds mi a finish off. Mi sista gwine bring yuh a cup of tea. Pick out de hair fah mi nuh," she said as she exited the room to finish off someone's hair in the bathroom.

The regulars were there, but there were a few faces Mrs Brown did not recognise. The women resumed their unfinished conversations. The dialogues meandered in various directions and were restarted and changed, as the women brought into the sanctuary, pieces of their lives that had weighted them down, during the past weeks and months. They asked Mrs Brown about her son and his new school, and the rest of her children. She told them of her satisfaction with the new school, and the child's renewed interest in learning. The mother told them that her son spent his spare time, in the grand ornamental red brick Carnegie Library building in the middle of their road, reading 'Biggles' and the 'Secret Seven' books. Often, these books were left lying around their small home. The younger children studied the pictures and words, improving their reading skills. This eased their guilt because they did not know a lot about books, or what or where to buy them with the competing demands on their limited wages.

The women's conversations continued to reflect the issues, that dominated their lives. Their children's schooling never seemed to go away or to be resolved in their exchanges. They discussed the many problems that weighed them down daily and found some answers because they had the space, to express, and share them. Yet, the mothers were unable to find practical solutions to their unending concerns, about their children's schools. The schooling of their children was their recurring nightmare. They seemed unable to come to grips with the education system, that was continually changing, and seemed aloof and disapproving of their children and themselves. The schools appeared as if they were unable to comprehend the community's simple requirements, for their children and their children's needs.

The women and men had brought their children to join them in England, as soon as they could afford to. The intervening years of separation had thrown up many issues between them. Many of their family patterns had changed, there were now new siblings and step-parents for their arriving children to adjust to. The long separation had made their children strangers to them, while new relationships had to be forged between the new family members. It would take time to iron out these issues, along with their schooling.

Desperately, the parents had hoped that schooling was the one area, that would make up for the separation issues. They had expected that by giving their children a good education, they would not suffer the deprivations they and past generations, had faced in the world of work. They wanted to break the unfortunate result, of their ancestor's enslavement over four centuries ago, as well as their present status in Britain as cheap unskilled labour doing the work, the white population did not want to do, but resented them doing.

At every turn, the women and men saw their aspirations for their children thwarted by the school system's, inability and apparent reluctance to cater for them. Without exception, all the mothers in the 'Women Place' had had issues with their children's schools. Like Mrs Brown, they sought to remove them from schools which they and their children felt, had not made enough demands on them. The women talked about and questioned the disproportionate numbers of their children in 'special schools', which did not and could not meet their children's needs or their expectations. Year after year, parents and the community had new issues to deal with, each decade brought a new twist in the school sector's response to their children.

As the parents and the community tried to deal with the excessive numbers of their children in 'special schools', the school system lobbed another boulder at them and their community. Significant numbers of pupils from the community and British born pupils were being removed from mainstream schools to off-site units and newly set up specialist units. The justification for their removal to these units was that these students were very disruptive in their classrooms and in the playground. As the years passed, more and more off-site units sprung up to relieve the mainstream schools of their children, thus increasing the parents' concerns and frustration.

As the island and the mainland community sought to challenge and build additional systems to school their children, to address the apparent inability of mainstream secondary schools, to educate their children, they faced new threats as the years passed. Next, significant numbers of male students were excluded from mainstream schools and found themselves on the streets. The community had to deal with the issue of exclusions as part of the school system's, persistent failure to accommodate and school significant numbers of their children successfully and keep them in the mainstream school environment. Subsequently, they also had to deal with their sons being arrested outside secondary schools and on the street, if they refused to allow the police to search them as part of the police's 'Stop and Search' policy.

The consequences of these exclusions were and would be disastrous for the island and the mainland community's advancement and future development. The education system in the United Kingdom appeared to be carrying out its historical and traditional role of maintaining the status quo. Historically, the school system had prepared the majority of white working-class students for manual work with some exceptions, while preparing middle-class students to carry out white and blue collar jobs. Many of the children of the wealthy occupied leadership positions in society because of their public school education. The British school system was demonstrating that a vast number of its schools did not have the skills to educate students who did not come from middle or upper-class backgrounds or come into the school system without middle-class skills and attitudes. The island and mainland students like their working-class peers were being prepared for manual work or no work at all.

To deal with the secondary schools' failure to educate significant numbers of their children for success, many African-Caribbean parents kept their children in education beyond 16 in further education colleges. They had hoped and prayed that their children would overcome the earlier obstacles to their secondary schooling, and gain the necessary skills and qualifications to move into higher education. They had to end the historical and traditional work roles assigned to them past and present. As the decades passed, many of the black school population left with more years of schooling, than many white working and middle-class children combined, but without the qualifications to advance beyond unskilled work. These students did not get the kind of jobs and monetary rewards that corresponded to the additional years spent in Further education and training. The mothers had to find a solution.

Diligently, the women sought and exchanged addresses of people who had been teachers back home, and were willing to tutor their children for a small fee. Small tutoring groups were set up in the small front rooms of the back-home teachers. Some parents encouraged groups of pupils from the same school, to come regularly after school to study together in their homes, to guarantee their exam success. Predictably, many of the teachers trained in the colonies had failed to get employment in Britain's schools, when they arrived qualified and full of hope because the British colonial teacher training institutions had not prepared them to teach outside the islands. Yet, white teachers trained in Britain would get jobs and quick promotion in the local schools soon after arrival. In many secondary schools in the islands and mainland at the time, up to half of the teaching staff was young British teachers or volunteers, one of those volunteers was Jeremy Corbyn. The education system's role in the colonies had kept and reinforced the white colonial hierarchy.

The experienced teachers from the islands and the mainland joined the army of black unskilled labourers, studied full or part-time to upgrade their qualifications, and in their spare hours, continued to practise their craft on their children and the islands' children, within the Black Supplementary School movement. A month later, a new woman arrived at the 'Women's Place', to have her hair experience the golden touch of Auntie Mackie. As the conversations returned to the mothers' discontent with their children's schooling, the woman volunteered information which made the women sit up and take notice. She told them that the pastor at her church, in Clapham was setting up a Saturday school for the children in the church hall. The Saturday school was also open to all parents, who wanted their children to get help with their school work.

She told them that there were many schools like these open on Saturday mornings in the larger cities and towns of the United Kingdom; her pastor had been to a meeting about them and had decided to set one up, in the church hall. She also told them that there were some back-home teachers in their congregation. These teachers and many more like them were wanting to use their skills, to teach the community's children. They were fortunate because the church in Clapham had a big church hall, to accommodate the Saturday school.

The Saturday school would teach maths and English well as the history of the Caribbean. The students would be guided by teachers, who had taught children back in the islands and the mainland with few resources. Many of these teachers had prepared numerous pre- and post-colonial students, for university entrance in America and Britain. The new member of the women's place told her audience that white teachers:

"A play wid di pickney dem, our back-home teachers nah play wid dem. Back home teachers expect dem fi learn, dem a go learn because dem know dat nutten nuh wrong wid di pickney dem brains. Di schools yah hab problems wid di pickney dem, an wid wi teachers to. Everything, wi do wrong fah dem, wi can't do right fah dem."

This was a God sent opportunity for the women. Unselfishly, this new member of 'The Women's Place' had given the mothers part of the solution they had wanted and had been desperately seeking since their arrival in the United Kingdom.

"It eena di Methodist Church in Clapham Common, di 35 and 45 bus pass dere. Yuh can also cum out a di tube station at Clapham Common wey dere is a tall clock. Yuh walk dung di road, yuh reach Clapham Park Road, cross in front of St Mary's church and go dung a Triangle Place, it lead eena Nelson Row at di side entrance, dat is wey it deh'. Ask anybody fah Clapham Methodist Church, an Pastor Andrews. A im a run di school eena di church all," she told them proudly.

The women vowed they would find the church and Saturday morning school. The supplementary schools, not only offered the mothers respite, that worked long night and day shifts to do household chores and shopping; they also challenged the British education system, to educate all its pupils equally. As the years passed, the children that attended these weekend schools began to improve in their mainstream schools, thus gaining more passes in the GCSE and national exams at the end of the school year.

The women grabbed the lifeline that was being thrown to them. It opened possibilities, for their children to enter the professional world in Britain, and shake off the legacy of their fore-parents' enslavement. Before and after slavery, a few white churches such as the Baptist, Methodist and Moravians had secretly helped a small section of the African population to learn to read and write. These Africans had passed on these skills to their family and community members. The Baptist church had fanned the flame of resistance, in the enslaved population in the cane pieces before 1838.

They had welcomed enslaved Africans into their congregations and had ordained some of these individuals to become preachers. These pastors had led the Emancipation movement, while members of the Baptist church had also provided land for Africans to set up free villages after they left the plantations. The Africans had appreciated this and had adapted, and joined these churches in their hundreds. These churches had also set up small schools, for the children of the liberated Africans after 1838. Once again in the centre of the ex-slaving empire, the nonconformist churches and their buildings had come to the aid of the community as they had done during plantation slavery. Now, the Methodist church was helping many children and their parents to achieve their educational goals in Britain. They were attempting to give them, the kind of schooling they were entitled to, that had been denied to them and their ancestors in the past by their enslavement, colonialism and now directly by the United Kingdom's education system after 1948.

More than four centuries later, in the heart of the colonial empire, in the United Kingdom, the islanders were forced to find supplementary schooling for their offsprings to ensure their school success, not generational and mass educational failure. They could not afford private education for their children now; unlike some white middle and upper-class parents who did not trust the state system to educate their children for the limited and well-paid jobs in society. To ensure that their children got the well-paid jobs, they paid for their schooling in prestigious and not so well-known private and public schools. They were paying for small classes and teacher attention to guarantee their children's educational success.

In the coming years, the black community would come to know that the British school system, had not only failed their children but also its own white working-class school populations too, especially the boys. The education system had not been designed for white-working class students, and it had not been intended for the descendants of ex-slaves, in the islands and the mainland or for their descendants invited to work and live in the United Kingdom, from 1948 onwards.

CHAPTER 13

The British education system
An illusion

The islanders and mainlanders' dreams and aspirations were shattered soon after their arrival in the United Kingdom. The colonial schools and their schooling had not prepared them for the reality of the mother country, its institutions or its people. The schooling of their children became their recurring trauma. As they collectively tried to overcome the bad dream, the system, again and again, torpedoed their aspirations for themselves and their children. Painfully, they had to learn and find solutions to the harsh realities they faced daily.

If their children were not reaching the standards they had expected and wanted for them in schools, these parents and their community soon learnt that they were not alone. As the years passed, they discovered that their fellow community members and their children that were educated and trained in British institutions in the mother country shared their daily experiences too. Rapidly, they began to realise that skin colour, and wealth was defining factors in the United Kingdom's education system and society; as it had been in their homelands. If schools had limited expectations for the community's children, likewise it did not have confidence in the black professionals coming into its ranks after higher education. Many Black and Minority Ethnic teachers were not welcomed into the vocation as competent professionals, who would naturally progress to leadership roles within schools with experience and staff development.

When Britain's history and relations with the non-white peoples of the world are analysed, it is not surprising that many teachers of African and Asian origin, career paths developed mainly outside mainstream classrooms and schools. Teachers from these groups had to work hard to stay in mainstream schools and make reasonable progress. Many Black and Minority Ethnic teachers found themselves on the periphery of the education system, teaching English or improving the educational attainment of African-Caribbean pupils in small groups. black and Asian teachers' jobs were funded by Section 11, monies allocated to provide supplementary teaching and learning for pupils from the islands and the Indian sub-continent at that time. Section 11 funding was the beginning and culmination of many Black and Minority Ethnic teachers' careers. They were always on the edges of the British school system.

When this funding was given directly to school head teachers, and governing bodies, rather than to the local education authorities, many African and Asian teachers found it difficult to remain in mainstream schools. Section 11 monies were used for other purposes and to pay the salaries of white teachers, the limited numbers of black and Asian teachers in the school system were becoming an endangered species. While the education system changed and meandered, in many directions in response to the agendas of politicians, political parties, businesses and influential white middle-class parents; again, Black and Minority Ethnic teachers bore the brunt of these changes. The reallocation of Section 11 monies and its eventual withdrawal, as well as the pressure for all-white schools in the inner cities by some working and middle class white parents, forced many black and Asian teachers, into daily and insecure agency work for privatised teacher recruitment agencies. Supply teachers got the problematic classes, white classroom assistants reported on them, and many head teachers used the opportunity to make their schools 'all-white schools' to attract middle class white parents and their children in the inner cities.

As marginalised professionals in daily supply teaching post, they would not challenge white teachers' promotion prospects in mainstream schools. Many white professionals wanted to work with and be managed by white professionals only. Hence the influx of teachers from Australia, New Zealand, South Africa, Canada and Europe. These teachers were welcomed into the teaching profession, and some progressed to senior positions, i.e. deputy and head teachers post as a matter of course. Australian teachers helped to teach the literacy and numeracy strategies borrowed from their schools by New Labour. The British establishment has consistently shown that both professional and manual workers from the white Commonwealth and Europe have always been their preferred option. The diminishing numbers of Black and Minority Ethnic teachers still in mainstream provision were forced to move from school to school seeking promotion after many, many years in the profession.

Head teachers and governing bodies were reluctant to promote the young and incredibly talented black British teachers coming into inner-city schools. These teachers had the required experience, exceptional professional development, excellent examination results, firm discipline and good relationships with their pupils, most of them from the Black and Minority Ethnic backgrounds, yet they were passed over for promotion. Newly trained white male and female teachers were promoted instead, to the fury of Black and Minority Ethnic parents and their communities. Helplessly, they watched as the skills and talents within their community were being destroyed by the institutionally racist British education system.

Political ideology and educational priorities had changed continuously, since the introduction of the 1944 Education Act. The act attempted to reverse some of the past injustices faced by most white working-class pupils who were schooled up to the age of 13 or 14, in elementary schools. The new Secondary Modern and later the Comprehensive Schools' responsibility was to attempt to end these inequalities and bring about more equitable education provision for all classes. Parents' occupational status and the ability to pay for their children's schooling in private and public schools would not decide the future of most of the school population. The act moved towards a more meritocratic system of schooling based on pupils' ability.

From 1965 to 1979, non-selective Comprehensive schools sought to create more equal education provisions for the school population. They did this by educating pupils from all social classes and abilities in the same school. However, this quest for equality in education delivery and outcomes were short-lived, it was overturned in 1979, by a Conservative government in the Education Reform Act, 1988. The

Act encouraged a return to selective and unequal school provision, pupils were to be tested at 11 years and placed in grammar or streamed in secondary schools, which disproportionately benefited the upper and middle classes. The incoming Conservative education minister and his 'Black Paper' supporters denounced comprehensive schooling. They argued that the comprehensive school model had not enhanced schooling. They also claimed that comprehensive schools, progressive teaching methods and 15,000 teachers were responsible for a decline in educational standards in Britain's schools, the model was gradually phased out by this government.

The Conservative government then introduced a conservative education agenda for schools, a national curriculum, revised teaching methodologies, funding to schools' governing bodies as well as a focus on teacher performance. They also introduced independent City Technology Colleges funded by the government. Teachers and head teachers were under scrutiny from the state and its inspectorate, OFSTED to conform to a revised philosophy of education, mandated teaching and learning targets and outcomes for schools. The relatively low numbers of Black and Minority Ethnic teachers in inner city schools and the country did not threaten, the incoming administration and school population. However, they were visible to those who wanted all white teachers and schools for their children in the inner cities. Therefore, it was inevitable that they would be perceived as part of the fifteen thousand ineffective teachers, that the chief inspector and newspapers told the public were responsible for a decline in educational standards in British schools.

Gentrification and property speculation in the inner cities would further add to the problems faced by Black and Minority Ethnic teachers, pupils and parents. A new government in 1997, resulted in a change in education ideology and policy once again. This government focused on improving the literacy and numeracy of all pupils in schools, objectives the immigrant communities, all parents and teachers welcomed and supported. The New Labour Prime Minister's mantra was Education, Education, Education. However, a closer examination of education policies and practices at the time, indicated an emphasis on the wants of middle class parents and businesses. These groups and the immigrant population had helped to bring New Labour to power after 18 years of Conservative administration.

The young white middle-class wanted schools for their children, in the inner cities because they could not afford private or public schools, or wanted them for their primary age children. Businesses wanted a share in the education sector, the New Labour Prime Minister duly obliged both. The privatising and restructuring of Local Education Authority services had started under the Conservative Government and was further expanded under New Labour from 1997. New Labour continued to dismantle the welfare state begun by the Conservative government and encouraged more business participation in education.

The New Labour Prime Minister's significant contribution to education, at the beginning of the 21st Century, was to continue to fragment state secondary schooling introduced by the 1944 Education Act, and administered by state institutions, i.e. elected Local Education Authorities. State secondary modern schools were created to meet the expressed demands of white working-class communities for decent school provision for their children after World War I and II respectively. Secondary modern schools catered mainly for working class pupils in working-class neighbourhoods and were from their inception the poor relations of the British education system. They were not created to deliver quality, equality and social mobility via schooling, but to maintain the status quo and be the source of manual labour for the society. Grammar, public and private schools, were designated to deliver social mobility via the school system. The Comprehensive school was an attempt by concerned educators to try to overcome this inbuilt and historic inequality within the education system.

Therefore, many students in secondary modern schools would always perform below grammar and private schools' students when measured on the same tests. The property boom in the inner cities was partly fuelled by parents moving to the catchment areas of grammar schools and 'good' primary schools. There was and is not enough grammar and well-resourced primary places for the whole school population; hence selection at 11 years for the limited number of spaces. State secondary schooling for the masses of white working-class students was only 44 years old when the Conservative Government passed the 1988 Act to halt the development of comprehensive education in Britain. They intended to provide more grammar schools places for their middle-class constituents and their children. The 11+ examination also conceded that ability was not only to be found in wealthy and the middle-class school pupils. But more importantly, it was an acknowledgement that the society had and was throwing away working-class talent and ability to its detriment. The 11+ and grammar school places gave the masses of bright working-class students the quality schooling they deserved.

In 1997, New Labour should have tackled the past and present structural inequalities in education. However, their conversion to 'the market economy' informed their policies in education. The Conservative government had sold off the utilities and the railways and had introduced limited business involvement in the running of secondary schools. Education and the health service were the only services left for New Labour to privatise to keep its new middle-class constituents and demonstrate its commitment to big business.

Instead, the New Labour Prime Minister used 'special measures' to place failing secondary schools into the hands of the business sector. He passed on the structural inequalities in the society's schools to 'middling capitalist'. Later other sponsors were sought. He justified his party's actions by saying that sponsored secondary Academies were a 'new' and ground-breaking way to raise the educational attainment of disadvantaged pupils in inner-city schools. The New Labour leader described the academies he created as 'a new chain of *independent* state schools'. New Labour was courting the business world, and many of the failing schools were taken over by them. The Prime Minister said at the time that these sponsors would bring the schools up to the standards found in successful schools. Historically, the society and its institutions had failed to tackle and find solutions to the inequalities inherent in the school system. Can businesses bring about these structural changes when they are profit driven and not welfare oriented? New Labour was putting the final nail in the coffin of the welfare state, the mechanism that had brought about secondary modern schools for working-class students in 1944.

OFSTEDs Dataview 2016 shows that the sponsored business academies have yet to deliver improved attainment for all disadvantaged pupils. Most of the schools that converted to non-sponsored academies were high performing schools, and they continued to be judged by OFSTED as outstanding schools, while the sponsored business academies continue to struggle. Twenty-seven per cent of these schools are judged by OFSTED as needing improvement, and eight per cent are judged as inadequate. The underperformance of many sponsored academies continues because the social class and ethnic composition of many of them remained unchanged, unlike the comprehensive schools which had sought to recruit pupils from all social groups. A freedom of Information request in 2015 to the Department of Education, stated that sponsored business academies were not the best or only route to school improvement. The debate continues, a Parliamentary Report in 2015 warned that government should stop exaggerating the success of academies and be cautious about drawing firm conclusions. Many Black and Minority Ethnic pupils are in business sponsored academies. Unequal access and outcomes to good quality schooling for many learners in schools in the inner cities was repackaged and delivered in shiny new buildings as part of the Public-private partnership (PPP) under New Labour and run by business people predominantly. However, the sponsored academies have succeeded in bringing some order and discipline into many inner-city schools, which will help them to raise education standards.

A Local Education Authority with a high percentage of pupils from Black and Minority Ethnic backgrounds failed its OFSTED inspection and was put into 'special measures'. Subsequently, the LEA was run by a private education company for a few years, another of New Labour's experimentation in education. A significant number of parents and the local community in the well-preserved Victorian suburb, in East Dulwich, did not support the business model and experiment in education pioneered by New Labour. East Dulwich and the LEA became the battleground for state schools versus business run schools. The parents and community wanted and fought for a community secondary school.The school would be accountable to them, the elected Local Education Authority and the community.

Business won easily, the parents got an Academy that was accountable first and foremost to the business people who ran it. Only new or converted academies was funded directly by the government. A primary academy recently opened, on the grounds of the former police station in East Dulwich and it is likely to become the feeder school to the secondary academy which in the future is expected to serve middle-class white parents and their children. Statistics from the Department of Education indicate that there is a growing trend in the sponsored academies' intake, away from working class to middle-class students in some areas of the country. The newly built primary academy in East Dulwich's intake is predominantly white middle-class pupils, and these students will move on to the secondary academy run by the same sponsor. If admission guidelines are not strictly adhered to, pupils from Black and Minority Ethnic backgrounds will find it difficult to get into the feeder primary school and later the secondary school. Black and Minority Ethnic teachers will have difficulty getting jobs in these academies because they are semi-autonomous and are not obliged to follow existing legislation and standard practices. Black and Minority Ethnic teachers feared marginally better under Local Education Authorities because they could be held to account for their employment practices using existing legislation.

Department of Education statistics in May 2017 indicates that 36 per cent of schools are sponsored business academies, 26 per cent are non-sponsored converted Academies, and 31 per cent are still Local Education Authority schools. However, most secondary schools are now sponsored academies, and they are out of the control of the elected Local Education Authorities. Tax payer's money goes straight into the hands of businesses. A local carpet businessman was the first to take part in New Labour's experiment, he has forty-one schools across London and is expanding his portfolio each academic year. The business community competed to get more and more schools for their individual collection from across the country. Newspapers at the time reported, and the police investigated claims that businesses sponsoring academies could get honours.

In March and September 2017, two trusts admitted they could not transform the educational attainment of pupils in their schools.

The Education Fellowship Trust and Wakefield City Academies returned 33 secondary schools to the Department of Education. The trusts conceded that they did not have the skilled personnel and organisation to raise the educational attainment of pupils by themselves. Today, special measures are also used in NHS trusts hospitals judged to be failing to provide quality medical facility and sound financial management. Time will tell if 'special measures' will be used to assist in the privatisation of the National Health Service.

The parental choice agenda of both political parties gave those it was intended for middle-class white parents, governing bodies and headteachers the opportunity to create 'good schools', in the inner-city to meet the needs of the incoming white middle-class parents. Good schools as defined by these parents were schools with all white teachers and pupils. They got the 'good' primary schools they wanted for their children in a very, very short time. Black and Minority Ethnic parents had stated their requirements too, good schools and education for their children from their arrival. However, their choice as parents was not acknowledged, the choice agenda was not intended for them. The only option available to these parents were the schools their children were already in, or they would have to find alternative ways to school their children for school success and social mobility.

In 2010, a Conservative and Liberal Democratic coalition came to power, they continued the policy of removing schools from the elected Local Education Authority's control. The new government's 'free schools' funded by taxpayers allowed founding groups, parents, teachers and community organisations to create and run schools. The application for funding for a 'free school', by the islands and the mainland's community Supplementary Schools coalition has not been successful to date. However, white middle-class founding groups and their communities got funding and buildings for their schools very soon after the policy was initiated. The wants of middle-class white parents and their children have always been a priority for all the political parties in the inner cities. It is not surprising therefore that many pupils from Black and Minority Ethnic communities continue to receive poor quality schooling and thus fail to meet the required GCSE grades for their age group.

The pro-middle-class policies of the three political parties acutely affected the small number of Black and Minority Ethnic teachers and head teachers still in inner city schools. Their exodus from many inner-city schools began in earnest. A primary school in East Dulwich, London, in the borough with an 80 per cent Black and Minority Ethnic school population became the target for an all-white primary school for the incoming middle classes. Previously, the school had catered for Black and Minority Ethnic pupils from the local area and the neighbouring boroughs because many black parents were always looking for 'good schools' for their children and felt this was a good school. The headteacher and some of the staff were from the islands and the mainland communities. The school was put in 'special measures' and reorganised after an OFSTED inspection. The few Black and Minority Ethnic teachers left in the school were systematically replaced by the new head teacher.

"Black is a dull colour", the head teacher barefacedly remarked to a black teacher in this school. Newly qualified white teachers replaced the black teachers, they had little knowledge or experience of the curriculum and pupils from other backgrounds in the transition to becoming an all-white school. They had limited knowledge and understanding, of the structure of the Literacy and Numeracy strategy introduced into the curriculum a few years before by New Labour. They did not know the difference between the religions of the Sikh, Hindu and Muslim children in their classrooms. Yet, they were fast-tracked as managers in the school, a policy encouraged by New Labour in most workplaces at the time. Eventually, with a few covert twists and turns to get around race equality legislation the school became an all-white school. Young white teachers were not as costly as experienced white and Black and Minority Ethnic teachers. The younger generation in all professions was more likely to be converted to New Labour's championing of the business sector.

The head teacher of the school in the well-preserved Victorian suburb, in East Dulwich, continued a trend that had swept across many inner-city local education authorities and would continue to do so in the 21st Century. The teacher unions were silent, especially the oldest teacher union in Britain, its general secretary at the time and officials became passionate supporters of New Labour's policies in education and trade unionism. New Labour's 'New Unionism' unlike the Conservative administration in the 1980s would not attempt to smash the trade unions and legislate away their power. Instead, the Labour Party, (New Labour) the child of the trade union movement co-opted many general secretaries and trade union officials to promote business and management interests at the expense of their subscription paying members in workplaces.

Most trade union officials were instructed to play down or side-step their member's legitimate grievances against management in workplaces. In 2010, it was stated in trade union headquarters in London by an official that only five representatives out of thirty in a large branch continued to support and promote their members interests during New Labour's 'New Unionism'. Blatantly, many trade union representatives (thugs) in trade union education centres, regional offices, headquarters and branch offices intimidated and verbally abused their members to implement and promote New Labour's reformulation of trade unionism. Confidently and arrogantly, they ridiculed, laughed at, blamed and silenced many of their subscription paying members for thirteen long years. The union representatives who continued to support the principles on which trade unionism was founded and regulated, in the 19th Century by exploited and oppressed workers were branded 'militants'. The militants had to be removed from the unions and schools to facilitate management programmes. The New unionism was the politics of the middle way, moderates, management and money. The refrain of the moderate trade union officials was 'take the money and deal and go' or live with the consequences. Black and Minority Ethnic teachers were advised to go and do supply teaching. Desperate union representatives would ask union members casually on behalf of LEAs "how much do you want, so and so got XX amount?"

The 'New Unionism' enabled the newly forming academies and management in many workplaces, to have a free hand to develop the pro-business and privatisation policies encouraged by New Labour. Established teachers' pay and working conditions threatened the academies' need for flexible pay and working condition to establish themselves; the trade union's hands-off approach would allow management to try to restructure professions and workplaces. Trade union policies also benefited governing bodies and management in schools in boroughs undergoing gentrification. Many governing bodies took the 'Devil' sent opportunity sanctioned by the trade union hierarchy in London, to replace their workforce, especially schools in the inner cities, to meet the wants of middle-class white parents for schools for their primary age children.

Segregation in school provision based on skin colour and ethnicity flourished during this period and have become the norm in inner-city schooling in Britain. White middle-class parents got the 'good' primary schools the 'parental choice' agenda should have given to all parents for their children in the inner cities. Businesses acquired schools for their portfolios, to become the biggest providers of secondary schooling with taxpayer's money, thus reducing the role of the elected Local Education Authorities. The sons and daughters of the wealthy continued to be schooled in the many renowned private schools in the well-preserved Victorian suburb, in Dulwich. The well-preserved Victorian suburb, in East Dulwich, became progressively white and middle-class.

The prolific and recurring research projects and Department of Education reports are a testimony to the state of British schools in the inner cities over the last 70 years. At regular intervals, the under-representation of black teachers and head teachers in British schools are routinely articulated in the press and at conferences; as well as the concern with black children's under-attainment which continues into the 21st Century. At the same time, ruthless government and trade union policies have facilitated the removal of the already limited numbers of Black and Minority Ethnic teachers from many inner-city schools. Many of these schools also have high percentages of Black and Minority Ethnic pupils, that are now being taught by newly trained white teachers who readily acknowledge, that their training does not prepare them to teach these pupils successfully.

This group have continued to underachieve when compared on attainment indicators with other Ethnic groupings. Many Black and Minority Ethnic students are enrolled in sponsored business academies, these academies have not convincingly shown that they can improve educational attainment for their students. Business sponsored academies are New Labour's experiment in schooling, they are not guaranteed to deliver effective schooling for all pupils. The British education system has not been adequately held to account in the past or in the present, for its failure to make available 'good quality' school provision for all pupils, irrespective of their race, class and gender.

From the outset, the representatives of the island and the mainland communities have had to challenge and redress the failure of the education system to school their children equitably; as well as reasonable promotion prospects for its teachers. Professor Gus John, an islander from Grenada, a former Director of Education in a London borough, and well-known community activists along with Rosemary Campbell, a former black head teacher, confronted the well-known secrets in the British school system. The reality was that those Black and Minority Ethnic teachers still within mainstream schools, had continually hit a glass ceiling when they sought promotion for deputy and headships, and other senior posts. They set up courses for Black and Minority Ethnic teachers to ensure their progression to leadership positions in all United Kingdom schools so that they could begin to change the school system for all pupils.

The black professionals within the education system did not allow these structural injustices to paralyse them, it made them work even harder to overcome them. They took up the challenge. Beryl Gilroy, Carlton Duncan, Winston Best, Norma Gibbs, Mrs Mannion, Mrs Thompson, Greta Akepene, Ken Noble, Charles Mungo, Basil Morgan, John Prince and others had torn down the glass ceiling. They defied the system and took their rightful place as headteachers in primary and secondary inner-city schools, after many, many years of teaching and working to advance equality of access and outcomes for all pupils in education.

Nothing had changed in the intervening four centuries, the community had to learn once again that they could not expect anything from the British school system and society, they would only succeed if they relied on themselves and their community organisations. They would have to fight for everything they wanted or were entitled to in the United Kingdom.

35 bus to Shoreditch
Photo: B.Ellis

AFRUIKA BANTU Saturday Supplementary school at the 1st August Emancipation Day celebrations 2017 Windrush Square, Brixton, London, in memory of Afruika Bantu (AKA Annette Blair) 11th September 1955 to 12th September 1999. Founder member of the Saturday supplementary school along with Brother Minka and community members.

CHAPTER 14

A Home of Our Own

The women tackled their housing problems head-on if their girl and boy children needed separate rooms and space for themselves to do their homework and entertain, it was the women who had identified these urgent needs. Jointly, the mothers sought solutions to their housing woes, understandably these issues dominated their discussions in the 'Women's Place', their sanctuary.

"Wi haffi tek a leaf outta di people from India and Pakistan's book. Dem get dem own house wid dem own communities, an dem set up dem shops and sell dem food, wi haffi do di same," said one of the women.

"But most a wi a dweet alreddi from di time wi cum yah. Ef wi did wait fah dem tiefing white landlords, and di council fi gi wi a place fi live, wi frozen bodies wooda all oba London's streets in di ice an snow. Wi wooda all ded by now," another stated.

"Mi sister pay dung on a lickle house in Railton Road, at di top a Brixton, near di market. It nah big, but wi all cotch up eena di house til wi can do better. A lot a wi people live eena di big mash-up houses in dat area, in Shakespeare, Chaucer, Spenser, Milton and Somerlyton Road an all dem roads in dat area. Dere is a lot a rundown house out dere fi pay dung on. Ef wi tink wi nice and wi a go skin up wi face and want a big house in dem white areas, wi a go wait til di good Lawd come," one of the women informed the gathering.

"Mi know smaddy from mi district eena Jamaica wha buy houses in Islington, North London long before, wi start come yah in di boat dem in 1948. Im buy some run-dung houses in Islington and rent dem out, an den di Labour government come and mash dem dung build flats ebery wey. Im mad yuh si. So yuh si wi a dweet it lang time", she said proudly.

"A tru di Labour government knock dung black peoples' houses afta dem buy dem and build flats, and den put dem eena dem fi pay rent", confirmed another woman.

"Mi fren live eena Derby eena di countryside, outta London. She nuh go pay dung on one of dem brand new house on a new housing estate, yuh fi si how dem treat har. She a outcast, di whites seh she spoil dem new estate, and dem all want fi sell up and move. Dem seh she shoulda a buy a old mash-up house in a Derby City Centre, wey di islanders an de Pakistani an Indians live."

"Dem do the same to the Indians and Pakistanis to. When di Indians and Pakistanis move in one street de whites sell up an move to di nex area. Dat is why many a di cities hab areas wey only Indians an Pakistanis live".

"Di same ting a happen to wi to," replied another woman.

"Look wha a happen, eena Balham, Clapham, Brixton, Stockwell, Battersea an mi sure a di same eena North, West, and East London. Is black and poor white people dat live eena dem big old run-down houses, di whites wid money lef lang time an gwan outside London. Wi a keep di areas warm fah dem and dem pickney, fah wen dem cyan afford the beautiful and expensive suburbs an waan fi come back."

"Mi pay dung on fi mi lickle house. It damp in places but di walls solid and mi hab windows an doors. Wen mi get money mi wi fix it up. Mi hab two tenants an dem rent help pay di mortgage," one of the women disclosed.

"An dat is how wi hab fi do it fah di time being, till wi caan do better an wi haffi help each odder."

"It nuh easy fi get a mortgage fram di building societies an banks, dem seh wi wages too small," another woman stated.

"A nuh dat is di reason, dem nuh want wi fi get above dem an get on. Soh dem seh wi cyan pay mortgage," confirmed another woman.

"Yuh haffi get it from di money people or di council. Dem charge more dan di building societies, but yuh haffi get di money from wey ever yuh caan mi seh because wi cyan live, unda bridges or in trees like di white people seh wen dem a cuss wi. Dem seh "go back eena oonu trees monkeys or go back a oonu country in di banana boat."

The women talked and gossiped about their trials and tribulations, at every gathering in between getting the hairdresser, to wash and style away their stressful lives. The mothers shared their news and experiences and kept each other hopeful and looking forward. They had found it hard to get used to the cold weather, but it was the cold and frostiness of the white population that they found hard to come to terms with. White people stared ahead and did not greet each other when they met or passed by in the inner cities. Their eyes and faces were always above your head when you looked their way. And if by chance your eyes caught theirs, they gave you a fixed cold and toothy grin.

You could go for days, without seeing the individuals that lived next door or lived in the same house. Everyone was busy working; money was the object of everyone's existence. In Africa, the Caribbean islands and the American mainland, people did not pass without greeting each other. They bid each other a good morning, day or evening. It was one of the traditions, the African slaves had kept alive during their years of servitude. After slavery, this African survival had flourished and become the norm in their small rural communities and in the towns and big cities. It is still so in the 21st century in the islands and the mainland.

The Africans acknowledged the existence of each other as an essential and critical human need. Children were taught to greet their elders and show respect, or the community would come down hard on them. The hours spent at work did not give them the desired rewards. The cycle was never-ending, more time at work to earn more money, that disappeared as soon as they got their pay packets and less time with family, friends, neighbours and community. The imposed isolation of the islanders and the mainlanders increased. The women took every opportunity, to unburden themselves when they met in each other's homes and at their sanctuary.

Mrs Cann told her story, everyone listened attentively. She had two young children living with her in the small flat in Herne Hill Road. However, she had five children back home with her mother that she had to send for soon. The three girls were growing up fast; they had left them seven years before. The boys would have to wait. The long separation concerned her and the effect it would have on the children back home. She worried that her daughters might not get on with their two younger siblings.

But before she could book their airfare, she had to find more rooms for her family. Her brother-in-law was in the same situation with a young family. They decided to pay down on a house together. It would have to be a large dwelling to house both families. They needed a home on two or three floors. The women in both families had been throwing their 'pardners,' so that they would have money put by if anything came up.

Fortunately, after much searching, they found a house on two floors with many rooms in Blue Post Hill, at the top of Herne Hill Road. It was a leafy area very close to Dulwich Railway Station. The house had a sitting tenant, and that had made it more affordable for them. The owners wanted to get rid of the house because of the sitting tenant.

The rooms in the house were huge. They would be able to divide some of them, so both families would have enough bedrooms, for the children here and those joining them. Mrs Cann and her family left the ground floor flat in Herne Hill Road, for their new accommodation in an affluent neighbourhood. It was promptly let to a Jamaican woman, her Ghanaian 'husband' and their two young children, Junior and Esi. Africa and its diaspora had come together in London, this would be the trend in the future.

The women talked to release their stress and worries; woman after woman shared their search for affordable accommodation for their families. One of the women informed her captive audience that she lived in a flat, in one of the houses with the green triangular covered entrances, in Herne Hill Road with her three young children. Her son was about to join her, her new husband and three younger siblings. She was worried about the effect it would have on him, she had left him with her mother eight years before. She hoped that over time the family would become one and that her son had not suffered adversely from their long separation. She had heard from a relative, that houses were cheaper in East London. There was a growing island and mainland community there. However, the Indians and Pakistanis had the biggest communities, much larger than the islanders and the white working-class communities who were in the process of running away to the suburbs.

Fortunately, for this family, the 35 bus from the bottom of Herne Hill Road, went directly to Leytonstone where their family members lived. Each weekend, they looked at houses family members had found for them. They were saving every penny to pay the deposit. Eventually, they found a three-bedroomed Victorian house with a 150-foot garden, in a row of terraces in a pleasant street. They borrowed and used their savings to pay the deposit. The mother told them they would be moving as soon as the papers were signed. She offered to keep in touch and let them know of affordable houses for sale in that part of London.

Next, Mrs Brown told her story.

"Mi did jus finish di night wuk an mi tek di pickney dem a school. Mi put mi hed dung on di pillow wen di Irish woman, Joan from di middle floor knock di door an caal mi. She seh dat a man from di council come fi si mi. She seh it important, mi put mi clothes back on an ax im fi cum in."

"Im cum in an seh sorry fi disturb mi, im nebba know mi wuk nights. Im seh di council get a letter from mi asking fah a council house or fah dem fi gi mi a mortgage. Im seh dem fine it hard fi undastan everyting mi write. Im cyan undastan mi crab toe, she said laughing. Im waan mi fi read it fah im. Im waan fi mek sure him undastan wha mi write. Mi dweet an im seh mi wi hear from di council eena couple of months."

"Well, after a month mi get a letter seh dem no hab no council house big enough fah mi fambly. However, dem wi give mi a mortgage, mi muss look fah a house. Dem seh mi mus hab a deposit fi pay dung. Mi haffi pay more fah di mortgage to because it cum fram di council. Mi write back, but dis time mi get one of di pickney dem fi write eena good English. Mi tell dem seh mi accept, an mi wi hab the deposit in t'ree months' time."

"A good ting hee, di pardner come a di right time. Now all mi haffi do is fine a house wi caan pay fah," she said half smiling and half crying.

The women understood her joy, they had been through the same emotions time and time again. They had experienced despair followed by delight when they managed to overcome, one of the many problems that dogged their lives in their adopted home. Consciously or unconsciously, the women were using their gathering at the 'Woman Place', as the family and community networks they had left back home, because of their imposed economic poverty, created by slavery and then colonialism.

Mrs Brown was not at work, she was 'sick' yet again. Her work and her children had worn her out. She took time off to recharge her batteries. This gave her more time with the family. When the children arrived home from school, their dinner was on the table. She could introduce the children to more dishes from back home, and she didn't have to rush off to work. The extra hours spent with her children were magical, she had forgotten the joy of being with her kids because now she had to work away from home. The children had been missing their mum too, back in the islands she had always been with them before and after school. During her 'sick' time, the children would encircle her, after they had eaten the delicious meals she had prepared for them. They would ask her to tell them stories about Jamaica, and her Jamaican childhood.

Mrs Brown was a good storyteller, she enjoyed the attention. As the children sat on the carpet of the small living room, their eyes and smiles widened, as they listened to the tales of their mother's childhood, and the family and community members they did not know. The children loved to hear these stories. One of the stories she told them year after year, was the story of her dead father, their grandfather. He had died just after she was born. She passed on the stories her grandmother had told her about her father. The children's grandfather was an influential man in the district where he lived. He had inherited a big wooden house on stilts, acres of land with sugarcane and a mill to go with it from his father. So, he was the 'big man' in the neighbourhood.

The small farmers in the district sold their cane and crops to him, he would take it to Kingston to sell in a big rumbling cart. He paid the farmers when he returned. Her father loved her dearly, she was his first child. Her grandmother had told her that a jealous neighbour had killed him, using Obeah and other unsavoury practices to get his land and his position in the community. The children wondered about many of the words in the story that they did not quite understand, but if their mother said so, it must have happened. They were sad that their grandfather had not defeated this man with his own Obeah concoctions, so he could be with them and their mother.

Secretly, they liked the idea that they were the grandchildren of their well-off, and once well-known grandfather. The youngsters could not wait for her to get to the part of the story, that scared them the most. They had requested it, even before she had started to tell the story, and she willingly told them.

One night, her dead father had come to her grandmother's house and took her because he loved her very much, and wanted to be with her always. He had hidden her among his family's gravestones, under a pile of leaves in the cemetery where he was buried. The children screamed at this incredible part of the story. They asked again and again if it was true. Mrs Brown swore to them it was so, her grandmother Edith and her neighbours would not have told her if it was not so. She informed them that in her childhood such events happened all the time, especially in the countryside, even if it did not happen nowadays.

Her tall and fierce-looking grandmother had searched high and low for her. The grandmother's sharpened machete had swung and chopped through the tall overhanging tree branches and bushes in the district, to look for her beloved grandchild. Eventually, after a long night's search and a chat with a wise community elder, her grandmother had found her among the gravestones of her father and his relatives covered with leaves. The children were amazed that such things could have happened. When their mother had finished her fantastic tale, the children asked for another, then another. The storytelling sessions continued until their bedtime each evening.

The children would hurry home from school, forgetting about the secret garden at the side of their school until her 'sick' holiday was over, and she had to go back to work. Mrs Brown took her 'sick' break each year, and the children waited eagerly for her hard to believe but enjoyable storytelling sessions, about her Jamaican childhood.

When the council had agreed to the mortgage, Mrs Brown and her daughter had gone to Brixton and the surrounding areas with large houses. As they entered, the estate agents' offices they looked at them and mockingly told them they could not afford the properties advertised within. They moved on to other more affordable areas that had island and mainland communities. Enthusiastically, the estate agents showed them many tumbledown buildings, without of shape walls and near collapsing chimneys. After weeks of walking and looking, they found a well-established estate agent on the corner of Grove Vale and Lordship Lane, in East Dulwich, a well-preserved Victorian suburb. They went in, and an elderly gentleman asked them to take a seat. He enquired how he could help. Mrs Brown told him her story, he excused himself and returned with a file of houses for sale.

"I think," he said. "I have just the house for you and your large family. It is more than your mortgage, but I am sure the lady selling it will negotiate. She wants to move to Wimbledon with her ageing mother soon," he said.

The next day Mrs Brown and her daughter visited the house with the estate agent, it was off Barry Road, in East Dulwich. The street was shabby, unlike tree-lined Barry Road, with trees from the church at the top to Peckham Rye park at the bottom. He showed her the house, the flat fronted Victorian house had a bay window, from the outside it looked small. Mrs Brown was doubtful at first as she stood outside in the small front garden. However, her doubts disappeared on entering the long hallway, grandly the stairs wound its way to the top floors as well as descending elegantly downstairs to the dining room, kitchen and a very tiny back garden. There were two good-sized rooms on the ground floor separated by a well-made folding wooden door. Next, they went down a flight of stairs to a medium-sized dining room with a small rectangular kitchen leading onto the yard. As they came out of the dining room; the agent opened a door leading to a considerable cellar running the length of the house. They gasped, Mrs Brown told him that her husband would love to work in it.

On the first floor, there was two more bedrooms, as well as the rear extension with a small bedroom and the only bathroom and toilet in the house. On the top floor, there were two little rooms, that had been converted into a small flat by the owner for her various lodgers. Mrs Brown was delighted, five bedrooms or even six if the living room's wooden door was kept closed.

The estate agent seeing her joy explained that from the outside the house seemed small, but the addition to the back of the house had given it more rooms. The Victorians he told her, had large families too, so these homes were built to accommodate them and their many children. He was pleased she liked the house, he wanted to have satisfied customers. He told her that when she was ready, he would try and get her a bigger house in Dulwich Village. However, the cost he said would be enormous, the house in East Dulwich, he noted had definitely been built for her and her family. Once outside she noticed the boarded-up buildings at the intersections of the road. On the corner of each street, there were boarded up houses or shops in a state of total disrepair. The area had seen better days. Next door the house was crumbling. However, at the end of the road, there was a main street with four buses serving the area and the City.

Barry Road had many families from the islands and the mainland. East Dulwich was affordable then and had become the home of many families, seeking a decent and reasonably priced home in South London. Some of the substantial houses on Barry and other roads were owned by islanders from Jamaica, Barbados, Trinidad and Tobago and their extended families. The streets leading off Sylvester Road ran to Lordship Lane, these roads had rows and rows of small to medium-sized houses, many islanders and mainlanders owned or lived in houses on both sides of Lordship Lane. It was their neighbourhood away from the islands and the mainland. Lordship Lane, the high street had many dilapidated shops, pubs and restaurants, it too had seen better days.

The estate agent assured her that although the surrounding buildings and area were run-down, there were two parks within walking distance. Dulwich Park and Dulwich library were at the top of Barry Road. There was another massive park at the bottom of Barry Road, Peckham Rye park which the children could enjoy. There were shops and a big market in Peckham about a mile away. The price of the house was more than the promised council mortgage, but he was sure a compromise could be reached. The deal was sealed, and Mrs Brown and her family moved to their big house in the 'well-preserved' Victorian suburb, in East Dulwich. Finally, the children had got their wish to live in a big house, but it did not have a large garden.

Mrs Brown could not wait for her next visit to the 'Women's Place', to tell them of her luck and to thank them for their helpful advice and encouragement. The women's desire for suitable housing, for themselves and their growing families, continued to be one of the leading topics at their meetings. They were becoming experts in the real estate market in the inner cities. Their reluctant hosts were leaving their properties in droves, to avoid living alongside and among them. It was not such a bad thing after all. They were building vibrant black communities in the inner cities, and the suburbs which would allow many of them in their retirement to sell these houses and return home, to grow food and flowers as many of them had done before their migration.

Michael McMillan's installation 'The West Indian front room' demonstrates the pride of his parent's generation, as their homes became their sanctuary and triumph over their 'reluctant hosts'. Their front rooms contained their family acquisitions, photo gallery, values, religion, and hard-won gains in the mother country. However, their children and grandchildren would not be able to afford the well-preserved Victorian suburb in the future. Gentrification and property speculation would drive up house prices beyond their reach, and return the 'well-preserved' Victorian suburb to the descendants of the Victorians in the 21st Century.

CHAPTER 15

Time for a change

Auntie Mackie told her captive audience, that she had tickets for a dance at the Ground Hound Hotel in Croydon, some miles from Brixton. It was being organised by Louie her former companion whom she saw now and again. Shrewdly, she gave them a rough idea about the attractions of the outing, before telling the women the price.

"Di Greyhound Hotel is di best eena dis area, wi all haffi dress up eena wi best fah dis yah do," she informed the women.

"Dere will be a t'ree course meal, wid entertainment an dance afterwards."

Proudly, she informed her audience that her nephew Derrick Morgan, the famous singer from Jamaica was coming over soon, and he would be singing his latest song at the event. She told them that her nephew had sung the independence celebration song in Jamaica in 1962, which had made him a household name on the island, and now among the islands and the mainland community in England.

"Im a try fi mek a lickle money, come an support im nuh," she begged.

Everybody will be there she told them. "Get your tickets before they go." The women placed their orders and were told that the tickets were £5.00 per person. The women gasped.

"A one week's wage dat," said one of the women.

Aunty Mackie assured them it would be worth it.

"Come, let wi go sidung an mek di white waiters walk afta wi an serve wi. It wut di money fi hab dem walk after wi. Mi gwine enjoy gi dem mi orda on di night. Mi no know none a wi dat ever get di opportunity before, so pay up and let wi go hab some fun wi dem facety white people. A caan just imagine dem face, wen dem si all a wi Black people dress in wi finery, an wi sidung an dem haffi serve wi," she said with a twinkle in her brown eyes.

Aunty Mackie's summing up of their experiences in Britain had been accurate. Day after day, they had taken the humiliation at work from their white work colleagues of all nationalities. In order, not to make things worse for themselves, they had taken on a non-confrontational role while gritting their teeth. They had to pick and choose their battles carefully because they were outnumbered. They had families to look after at home and children who were waiting to join them, elderly parents waiting each month for the small amounts they sent them. These responsibilities were their priority at this moment in time.

They would wait for the right time, to let these spiteful people in their mourning attire know they were not afraid of them. The women left the hairdressing salon with renewed enthusiasm. The forthcoming dance at the Greyhound Hotel in Croydon had revived their spirits. They began their preparations for the big night out. Aunty Mackie had carefully planned how to sell the maximum number of tickets. After all, she knew the state of the women's finances, and the responsibilities they had within their families. Most of the women had husbands or men living with them, but this did not mean they were 'kept women' without money worries. She knew the opposite was often the case. She told them as they left that they could give her a little each week, for the tickets because the big night out was three months away. The women appreciated the gesture.

Mrs Brown ordered a ticket for herself and her two eldest daughters. She wanted to show her appreciation for the help they had given her, with the youngest children over the years. The following week after leaving the children at the Methodist church in Clapham Common and paying the small fee; the women did their food shopping. Next, they walked to Bon Marche and Morley's stores respectively, on Brixton Road to see if they could find some reasonably priced fabrics to make suitable dresses, for their big night out since their arrival in England.

After much deliberation, they found some fabrics and patterns to make their outfits. They set off for the Methodist Church in Clapham to collect the children. Some of the mothers and their children took the bus to East Street Market, a street market located between Walworth and Old Kent Road, to do their weekly shopping and look for some moderately priced materials, for their dresses. The women had also used East Street and Petty Coat Lane markets to buy some of the necessities and little treats for their family members back home. At Christmas time, these packages were dutifully sent via the post office to family and friends. To the women' joy, the 35 and 45-bus routes went past the markets and shops.

The outing dominated the women's lives in the coming weeks. They fussed and changed their minds repeatedly about the dresses, jewellery, shoes and hairstyles they wanted for the occasion. They would need dressmakers, to sew their party clothes because they could not afford the store prices, and the women at the 'Women's Place' again had the answer. The women directed Mrs Brown and her daughters to the home of two mature sisters from Barbados, who had been in the country for many years. They had worked in various clothing factories in the East End of London from their arrival; making clothes for some of the Jewish garment factory owners around Commercial Road. After paying down on a three-storey house in Dalylel Road, Stockwell they had the space to start working for themselves, sewing the community's clothes in their later years.

The backroom's wallpaper was frayed and peeling. The fading paint could not revive the antiquated wallpaper that had served its time and usefulness. The old and shabby room was packed and overflowing with fabrics in tattered and threadbare wrappings. The age of these worn and torn coverings signified the clientele's preference, for the newer materials and fashions in the intervening time. Multicoloured buttons encased in clear bottles and containers, snuggled between mountains of fabric wrapped in crumpled paper. Colourful snippets of cloth and thread littered the floor covering, worn away by the pounding feet of the dressmakers and their clients. The noisy, abrupt stops and starts of the sewing machines, wiped out the ticking of the mantelpiece clock and its chimes. Sunlight streamed in through the curtainless window on the outside wall.

All day long, the electric light flickered and watched the comings and goings of the customers. It lit the dark space, until the weary dressmakers pushed aside the tattered bags with their half-finished garments, and turned off their ageing machines until the morrow. Slowly, they cooked their evening meal before watching television followed by sleep; to be prepared to meet the many women that would bring more fabric to sew.

The eager customers introduced themselves, they waited modestly for the signal that they would be admitted into the select, the wise and experienced circle of the sisters, Vera and Tassie. The women were twins, but not identical. Time had shaped them, one was tall and slim with dyed auburn hair and very white skin. The other's ageing body spread out across the clattering sewing machine. Vera always sat on a chair in front of her sewing machine, her dyed brown hair made it hard to guess her age and height accurately. Maybe, they were pensioners or very near that age. They were not Ebony. They were white Barbadians whose great, great grandparents may have gone to Barbados, as the first British settlers to attempt to tame the interior of the Barbadian wilderness, in the first half of the 17th century to plant tobacco, hoping to make their fortunes.

In 1625, British sailors had investigated the island of Barbados and had settled on it by 1627. The Spanish had ignored the island in the 1490s either because it was too small or possibly because of the noises that emanated from it which frightened them. So, later it became the main colony in the Caribbean for the British planters and government who developed crop and plantation slavery rigorously and exported it to their colonies as they seized islands from their rivals or bought land on the mainland. The indentured servants and pirate adventurers armed with the tobacco plant had hoped to make fortunes so that they could join, the ranks of the nobility and government officials, on the island and at home. But over time, the white lifeblood of these two women's ancestors had mingled with the bloodlines, of the enslaved Africans, and they were the result.

The two women although white in appearance was part of the island and mainland community in London. They were not members of white British society because their strong Bajan accents gave away their ancestors' past association with the Africans, they had enslaved. Happily, these two women mingled and served 'the back home' communities in Brixton, and the surrounding areas, who appreciated and welcomed their skills, talents and wisdom. Their Bajan accents and birth made them Caribbean citizens, and they provided a safe space and chit chat for a few hours, for their fellow islanders away from their distant homes, in cold and wintry London.

Mrs Brown and her daughters gave their parcels of fabrics to the dressmakers. Vera inspected it for quality and ease of sewing, then she took out her little book. She wrote their names and measured each one professionally. The small party felt relieved, as the expert dressmaker accepted them as one of her own immediately. As she took the mother's measurements, she said, Mrs Brown "you have a beautiful pair of breasts, flaunt them, flaunt them she told her, in her distinctive Bajan accent. If I had them, I would flaunt them," she said as she looked down at her flat and sagging breasts.

She wrote down their measurements and then looked at the fabrics they had given her.

"Lovely, lovely", she said in her musical Bajan accent.

"When yuh all want it," she said.

"In three months' time," they told her.

"A hab wuk for a lot a people going to a dance in Croydon," she told the women.

"Wi a go to," they replied.

She asked them if they had a style in mind for the dresses. They showed her the patterns they had rummaged through the cabinets in Morley's department store to buy. She took the Vogue patterns and told them that next time they wanted dresses sewn, they should bring a picture. She and her sister, she said could look at a picture of a dress, and cut it out free hand and it would save them money. The sisters had done their apprenticeships with highly skilled dressmakers in Barbados, in their youth. This had given them a good grounding in dressmaking. They arrived in London from Barbados in the middle of the 1950s, they had come because the United States government had closed the door to Caribbean migration, with its Immigration and Nationality Act of 1952. They like many who wanted to escape the poverty of the islands and the mainland, and could no longer go to the United States, accepted the British government's half-hearted invitation to come and rebuild Britain along with the Irish and other Commonwealth peoples, at the end of World War II.

Many of Tassie and Vera's immediate family members had migrated to the United States before 1952, including their eldest sister and they, were in regular contact with her. Vera and Tassie had frequent visits from her and her children. Annually, at Christmas time, the sisters prepared a parcel for their family members in New York, with the little delicacies from Barbados that they could get in Brixton market. In her later years, Tassie went to live with her niece in New York, leaving Vera alone in the two-storey house. The community in London rallied around her. The Caribbean community in London was now the sisters' new family, and they acted as mothers and aunties to the younger generation, and they were highly respected and valued until Vera's death.

Vera instructed them to return in two weeks' time for a fitting. They were pleased with all the things they had done that day, and especially with their new dressmaker, she would become part of their family in the years ahead. Mrs Brown did not visit the 'Women's Place' in the coming weeks. She had a lot of expenses. The mother was saving for her next hair appointment, the dance and to pay the dressmaker's bill. She sent her weekly instalment to pay for the tickets with her eldest daughter and her 'pardna money' to Auntie Mackie's sister. Aunty Mackie ran her hand through the girl's thick knotty and coarse hair and said.

"A wi gi yuh a beautiful hairstyle fah di dance, ef yuh mek mi straighten it."

The girl giggled and gladly agreed.

CHAPTER 16

The dance

The roof, walls and floors of the picture painted house, heaved under the weight of the hairdresser's generously proportioned clients. These women would sparkle and stand out tonight. Women from near and far converged on the squashed terrace. Aunty Mackie had sold tickets to anyone that entered her salon. The floorboards creaked and sagged, as the sprightly hairdresser barked orders in all directions for the women to sit still, or to sit up, as she speedily curled and piled hair on top of their heads, in the most expert way. She had reached the peak of her profession, she sculpted the women's heads, but more importantly, the hairdresser was their makeover artist, they knew she could give them the look they had always wanted.

"Whe oonu lef it fah di day a di dance fi do oonu hair. Oonu nebba hear bout forward planning. Everyone, a oonu a tink di same. Di Lawd gi mi ongle one pair of hands like oonu. Mi cyan do di impossible. Oonu know today gwine busy. Oonu expect mi fi get all di people mi sell tickets to redy fah tonight. Mi haffi get redy to. Ef oonu hair done dis yah day oonu lucky," she said flagging under pressure to do the impossible.

Adeptly, she fixed the women's' hair and hurried them out of the house, to prepare for the dance. As she steered the last woman out of the house, she asked her to stop at the railway arches at the end of Herne Hill Road. She was to tell Mr Ricketts the garage owner, to send one of the men with a car for her at 7.30pm.

Mr Ricketts, the proprietor of Ricketts' Garage, had joined his parents in England as a young man in 1957. They came from Guyana, his father had told him after he had worked here and there without direction, to get a profession. His father had asked a white mechanic in Battersea near their home to give his son a try, he had agreed when he realised that his apprentice might bring in much-needed trade from the new and growing community. The youth had reluctantly taken his parents' advice, the hours were long, and his clothes and body were greasy at the end of each day. It was not the profession he had dreamt of when he left the mainland to join his parents. The young man had stayed in the greasy business because he realised that in the future, he could set up on his own and earn more than the pocket money, he was getting each week. He stayed with the white mechanic for five years and in that time, built up a small clientele from his community.

As Railway stations closed in the aftermath of the Beeching Reforms of 1963, many of the railway arches were leased to private individuals and businesses, as this would earn British Rail an income. Mr Ricketts rented one at the run-down end of Herne Hill Road. He set up his garage with a few youths who had some experience, of fixing engines of all types back home. He was never short of business, as more and more of his community bought the kinds of cars they could afford, which meant they needed his skill and expert knowledge. Soon, they were driving the worn and battered vehicles the white population had disposed of, with the help of Mr Ricketts and his expert staff.

The grey-suited doormen in top hats and tails looked at each other in horror. They stared in disbelief at the half-battered wrecks pulling up in front of the entrance of *their* hotel. Any hopes of a tip faded. The state of the transport in front of them was a testimony to this. Inwardly, they fumed, they were being humiliated. Why should they be expected to attend to these people without the faintest hope of any recompense for their mortification? Why had these people turned up on their shift, forcing them to acknowledge and attend to them?

Eager, to start their costly evening, the paying guests waited for what seemed like an eternity, before the doormen came to their cars. They had expected their response, it was their everyday experience. They had paid for the service. They could have left their vehicles and walked into the elegant hotel reception, but they would be greeted and brought in as paying customers. Tonight, was their night and no-one would overlook or disrespect them.

And so, they stayed in their wrecks. They had paid for the whole package, and they would not be shortchanged. It amused them that their presence had disconcerted these pompous and pretentious doormen. They were ready for the challenge, they would prolong their anguish. They would make them feel as uncomfortable, as they had often been made to suffer in places like this, and in their workplaces. The stalemate ended, when the grey-clad employees realised that the passengers in the wrecks and their drivers, had come to be serviced, and they would not budge. They consoled themselves that their association with, the wrecks and their passengers would be very brief and short-lived.

Mechanically, their elongated arms stretched far beyond themselves and reached out, and opened the wrecks' doors without any contact or contamination. Their artificial and welcoming smiles hid their clenched teeth and their anger. Their nostrils flared and inhaled the disagreeable scent of the occupants. Swiftly, they ushered them into the hotel's reception to be processed by their subordinates.

The clientele glided into the Greyhound Hotel's entrance hall and became the people, they had wanted to be for centuries. They and their ancestors had stood in the corners of the great houses in the islands, the mainland and stately homes in England, and had watched their top and tailed masters and mistresses enter ballrooms bejewelled and in their best. They had served them, during the evening and had withdrawn from the glittering rooms, without the slightest recognition or acknowledgement. Now, it was their turn, and it had cost them. They were the proud and noble descendants of their African motherland. Their formal dress and posture mirrored the marble and chandeliered reception of the Grey Hound Hotel. Their warm, friendly smiles and ease of manner momentarily arrested the frown of the white reception staff, as they were thrust into their care by the surly grey doormen.

Tonight, was their night. They were young and carefree again, and they were about to relive the gaiety and delights of their past lives in the islands and the mainland. At home, with very little money, the weather and atmosphere had made it easy for them to feel glamorous and elegant. But, the frostiness and bleakness of their adopted home had fleetingly subdued their jolliness and zest for life. They would reclaim it tonight, in this modern and magnificent building. They would banish the humiliation of their workplaces; their meagre wages, their cold and cramped housing, their constrained ambition to excel and release their restricted abilities and potential in all spheres of life, in the United Kingdom.

This evening, they would be themselves, and it didn't matter if they threatened those who had been paid to wait on them. The revellers would dazzle these elegant surroundings with their style and flair. The women glided across the reception into the banqueting room, their bright sequined dresses, shoes and piled high hairstyles astounded and puzzled the hotel staff and onlookers. The mirrored reception entrance reflected their grace and sophistication. The men showed off the casual, stylish, lightweight attire of their homeland, while others chose the black and white top and tails, they had longed for in their youth but could only now hire for the night. The radiance and brilliance of the assembled people dazzled but outraged those who were about to serve them. Tonight, they had come of age, and their celebration would banish the bleakness of their existence since their arrival in the United Kingdom, momentarily.

The paying guests waited for the attendants that moved along the long rows of banqueting tables to serve them. The white serving staff wore the impenetrable smile of the Mona Lisa. The eyes of the waiting staff and the paying guests did not, and would not meet even for a fleeting moment. Such familiarity could not and would not take place. Throughout the evening, the undeclared war that had started at the entrance of the hotel by the doormen would be maintained and sustained. The paying guests understood the game and savoured it. They prolonged giving their orders, as the waiters hovered about them, they reordered and changed them, to experience the sense of power that had been taken from them since their arrival. They requested more and more drinks each time a waiter appeared, they kept them running, and they enjoyed this very, very fleeting moment of equality and the power that only money could give them.

The line of black and white clad servers walked along what seemed to them a never-ending row of overdressed and arrogant black people, 'fish' Madam, or 'steak' Sir, they said between clenched teeth, while plates landed on the tables in front of them with a thud. The contrived innocence of the partygoers prolonged the waiters' agony as they briefly forgot their orders forcing them to extend their stay. Finally, the small round plates with chocolate cake and wobbling cream flew onto the tables and slid between the paying guests. The skirmish was not over yet.

The paying guests held their own, and the showdown continued fiercely, as it had begun when the assistants tried to collect the empty dishes. The entrances and exits to the rows of tables were tightened, as the servers squeezed in and out of the tiny spaces bruising and scratching themselves, as they collected the empty tableware. Their bodies and egos were battered and bruised. The patrons had made their point, the hotel staff had got the message, they would not pay to be insulted and disrespected. Then, they turned their attention to the rest of the evening.

Graciously and effortlessly the men, women and children moved effortlessly onto the dance floor. The smooth, slick music of the islands and the crooning voice of Derrick Morgan would remove the disagreeable taste, left by the unnecessary confrontation with the hotel staff. The beverages had heightened their senses, as they moved to the familiar sounds, words and beat that was buried deep in their consciousness. The soothing sounds of the music took them back to the wholesomeness, of the sun-soaked islands and the mainland, where their communities had tried to block out the pain of their past hardship and servitude with music and their energy.

Their resistance and shared victory against the hotel's staff attempt to deny their presence and humanity, reignited in them the struggles of their ancestors, as they had fought to end their enslavement. The night's unfolding drew the partygoers together, to manage the undeniable turbulence that awaited them in their workplaces and society in the future. Temporarily, they were victorious, collectively they had triumphed over the hotel staff and their reluctant hosts.

CHAPTER 17

No Irish, no blacks, no dogs

Tired and worn out by the night's events, the staff at the Greyhound Hotel had vowed that they would never be exposed to another Saturday night like this one, never again would they serve crowds of Nigger pleasure seekers. They would forgo the money, to protect themselves from the indignity of such encounters. They had suffered unimaginable humiliation, having to wait on and serve those presumptuous black immigrants. The Negroes had humiliated them beyond belief. They had expected them, waiters with white skins to wait on them at tables, serve them drinks and escort them out of those ghastly wrecks, after bedecking themselves in the most garish colours and modes of dress. Why had the hotel's management allowed the bloody roles to be reversed in this hotel? The Blackies should have been serving them, as they had done for centuries in the great houses and on the sugar plantations, as slaves.

They took comfort from the present state of affairs, they would not have to live with, eat or sleep, in the same houses as the Blackies. Those formidable landladies had got it right. Like an army, they had squashed the impertinence of those who thought they could ignore the imperceptible colour bar and mix freely with people with white skins. Those no-nonsense notices in the windows, no Irish, no blacks, or no dogs had maintained the colour bar, the only advantage they as poor working-class whites had in their fatherland.

Their children were being swamped in local schools, by black and Asian children, and now they were being threatened in the social sphere. The 'white working-classes', had to stick together in the face of the threat posed by the hordes of non-white peoples', that had been allowed to flood the country, in recent years. Yes, the white working-class population were destitute, they lived in the ghastliest conditions and food had been scarce since the end of the war. Their children had been given the most basic schooling. They had been denied secondary education, for centuries because the ruling class believed that working-class children, could not benefit from an academic education and training. The discriminatory education system and structured class society had given their daughters and sons, the opportunity to be servants and footmen in the houses of the rich and powerful before and after the two world wars. White working-class people were discriminated against in their fatherland because they did not have money, land or power.

However, they had one consolation, thanks to the newly arriving black immigrants. The blackness of their skin emphasised their 'whiteness' and natural advantage, this would not change. They were white, and the colour of their skin had set them apart from them and their varying shades of creamy coffee through to Ebony. Their defences would be reinforced against the incoming Negro threat. They would stand firmly together in their white skins. Skin colour would be the marker, in their fatherland, where birth and wealth fixed one's place in society. The blacks might have been invited by the business people and government to come and work here, but they had not been consulted, and if they had been asked they would not have agreed.

Yet, it was the ordinary working people, who had to mix with them and was in danger of losing, the only symbol of power they now had in their fatherland, their 'colour'. The 'Toffs' lived in their big houses in the towns or in the countryside. The blacks had been their slaves and servants, on their estates and plantations in the colonies. Now, they were inviting them here to work for less money, therefore undercutting working people's wages, as well as taking their jobs and forcing down their pitiful take-home pay and their social conditions even further.

It was the business owners who would always benefit from the incoming blacks and Asian workers, at the expense of all of them. Deep in their hearts, working people knew they should forge bonds with the newcomers, against those who had in the past exploited them both mercilessly and would continue to do so in the future. But, unfortunately, history and circumstances had prevented them and had made them hold on to the last residue of power left to them, their 'skin tone.' It had become imperative to uphold their 'status' as the poor relations of the ruling classes in their workplace and in every other sphere to maintain their self-worth and self-confidence.

The hotel workers, heaved a sigh of enormous relief as they unceremoniously closed the banqueting doors, on their unwanted guests. As swiftly as they could, they ejected them from the hotel's reception, into the array of old wrecks that had degraded the front drive of the hotel's entrance. They cleansed themselves and the hotel of the contamination that had taken place.

The 'Women's Place' buzzed with excitement as the women recalled their night out at the Greyhound Hotel. It was a good outing. They had felt magnificent, even though the hotel staff had disrespected them from the moment of their arrival. However, they cherished the dream that there would be more outings like this one, to come together and forget the stresses and strains for a few hours. At the next gathering at the 'Women's place,' one of the women again reminded them of their outing a few weeks before.

"Auntie Mackie, a wen is di nex dance at di hotel, mi a go pay dung on mi ticket right now, tell Louie mi redy a redy," a woman giggled.

They all nodded in agreement. The night out had temporarily lightened the hardships they experienced daily among their 'reluctant hosts'.

"Yuh nephew Derrick Morgan mash up di place wid dem riddims. It tek mi right back a yaad man," said another finishing the dance she had started at the hotel.

"Mi did enjoy di dance. Mi nebba go on di dance floor once, but mi orda mi meal. Mi scrutinised de faces of di waiters, an mi haffi squeeze mi big toe eena di floorboards to stop mi self from bussing out a laff," her sister confided to her audience.

"Di agony pon dem faces wen dem si all wi gracious ladies and gentlemen dressed up and looked so elegant, dem cyan believe it. Dem nebba know dat black people coulda dress up so, an cyarri it off like queens and kings."

"Di real agony fah dem was wen dem haffi serve wi, put di plates in front of wi. Den dem haffi clear away wi dishes an scrape off wi lef obas. Dat's was wha hat dem di most," she grinned.

"But dem shoulda si it as a business. Mi nuh know why dem a skin up dem face because wi a put money eena dem pockets. Mi wi serve anybody ef it a put money eena mi pocket," sighed another woman.

"Dem white people funny bwoy," laughed another.

"Dem tink a one-time monkey a go waan wife. Dem nebba know dat eena slavery when dem treat wi ancestors appalling dat one-day wi wooda come an save dem country. Yuh si afta Hitler mashup dem country, dem same one haffi caal wi fi cum and help dem rebuild this thankless country, wen dem couldn't get enough of fi dem people. Mi gwine seh it again, a nuh one-time monkey a go waan wife."

The women could have continued discussing the encounter with the reluctant workforce at the hotel. However, they were back into their allocated slot, as mothers, wives, companions and workers. They had to put aside those challenges until the next time. They had more pressing problems to resolve. The pressures of surviving in a cold and bleak country, along with the cold grey-clad and dowdy population were now their main worry. The reality of their situation haunted them. The cold cramp rooms they lived in, had as many people as they could take. This was not what they had left the islands and the mainland for. They had envisaged a better life in the mother country. One of their migration goals was to improve their living conditions substantially. However, their living conditions now were worse than the dwellings they had lived in before their migration.

At home, they had lived in small rooms in tenement yards and board houses on the hillsides in the country districts, but they had the outdoors to compensate. During the day, they lived and worked under the shading Guango and fruit trees or on their little verandas protecting them from the glare of the sun. In the freshness of an evening, they stood by their fences and gates and talked and laughed with their neighbours. These were the memories and events that would help them to withstand the trials and tribulations they were now going through; and from which there seemed to be no escape. If they could, they would gladly return to their former homes which at the time, they had failed to adequately appreciate and value.

They wanted enough bedrooms for their girl and boy children and for themselves as parents. Their appeals to the local councils for housing came to nothing. They were appealing to the very people who did not want to associate or mix with them. They did not want their neighbourhoods, degraded and their estates tainted with black tenants and their unpleasant cooking smells. White working people wanted to be with their own kind and colour. They did not want the blacks in their backyards. As a result, the mistreatment and assault on them, from all sections of British society would only serve to strengthen them, to do their best so they could return home within five years. They would have to leave their children with the knowledge, skills and determination to continue to improve their lives.

The black community had learnt valuable lessons from their reluctant hosts, and so they bonded in their small neighbourhoods to strengthen themselves, against the hardships they knew were awaiting them if they remained in the mother country.

CHAPTER 18

The sanctuary

The 'reluctant hosts' had slammed the door in the faces of the invited guests at their arrival. They were now adrift, this time in poor and hostile inner-city neighbourhoods. The citizens and the weather mirrored their deprived, run-down and unfriendly surroundings. They huddled together, to produce the warmth that was withheld from them by their icy hosts and the weather. Daily, the premeditated resentment and vindictiveness of the population forced itself into their everyday lives, invading their every thought and action. They had to begin to break down the hatred around them, so they drew on their inner strength and their community's resourcefulness. They had been here before. During slavery in the islands of the Caribbean and the South American mainland, the Africans had built invisible fortresses around the cane pieces, their provision grounds and huts on the high ground of the estates and plantations. They had to do this to retain their African heritage and their physical survival.

Centuries later, they would need these invisible and defendable fortresses once more in the cold and inhospitable mother country. During slavery, the provision grounds, the huts on the compounds, hillocks, and the mountaintops had been their sanctuary. Now in this cold and foggy land, they had to find safe havens to heal and shield them from the onslaught of a selfish and changeable climate and people. These sanctuaries would not be sacred temples, cool watering places or the quiet of distant mountaintop retreats to contemplate their predicament.

In the cane pieces, the enslaved Africans had sung spirituals as well as the half-remembered songs and clicks of their mother tongue. These spirituals and the rhythm of their toil temporarily blocked out the insanity of plantation slavery. The changing shades of the misty blue mountain peaks in the distance, offset by the sun's rays had eased at intervals, the mental and physical blows that bombarded them at the hands of the enslavers, overseers and drivers. More than four centuries later, in the unwelcoming mother country, they had to retreat into their evolving churches, dwelling places, eating and drinking places as they had done in the islands and the mainland. However, it was their newly acquired shabby and cramped houses, that sheltered them from the lingering contempt of their reluctant hosts, and gave them the physical and mental warmth they so desperately needed.

The 'Women Place' in the row of picture painted houses, was the refuge into which the women forged the bonds of friendship and community to take control of their and their family's pain, sorrow and loss as they were hurled at them by their malicious hosts. Daily, they had to fend off the hatred and spite of those who did not want them in their country. The slenderness of the hairdresser's waistline contrasted starkly with the sprouting midriff of her customers. Auntie Mackie knew that when the women descended on her, she was expected to do more than wash, massage and style the heads over which she held sway. She was the person that fixed their hair, the listener, the therapist, facilitator and friend. Their 'worries' and isolation firmly implanted in the heads that she tweaked and shaped continuously.

Unconsciously, the women hoped she would wash away all that troubled and threatened them. The women's fears were the community's concerns, and they did not and would not go away, daily their anxieties multiplied as their destructive hosts viciously flung more insurmountable 'ones' at them.

"I can fix oonu hair, but mi cyan fix oonu troubles. Wi all eena dis together, mi hab mi own troubles to. Wi hab fi find ways outta dis together, as dem a get bigga and bigga ebery day," the hairdresser told the women wearily.

Then she addressed the assembled women.

"Oonu know wi Sister Sally. She is di big boned mixed-race African an Indian ooman wid nuff hair from Trinidad. Lawd, oonu cyan imagine di trouble she in. She hab one almighty problem wid har ongle son. She jus bring im oba a few years now, im finish school an a wuk mi seh. Im a get a good trade, im apprenticed to Mr Ricketts di mechanic dung a Herne Hill Road," she informed them.

"One evening im a cum fram di garage wen di police dem stop im, an haul im eena dem van. Dem step eena im back, an im face. Eena di van dem beat im til im blak an blue. Wen dem reach di police station, dem drag im outta de van and drag im eena di station fi charge im fah obstructing dem."

"So wha im do fi mek dem stop im?" asked a woman.

"Sister Sally seh, dem seh dem a stop an search im because it is di law. Di police caan stop an search anybody dem like. But dem ongle stop black men and bwoys. Dem seh dem ax him fi tun out im pockets, im refuse an so di trouble start. So dem haul im eena di van fi go lock im up."

"So wha mek im blak and blue," asked another woman.

"Di police seh wen dem a put im eena di van im a resist arrest, so dem haffi restrain im. Dem chuck im eena di cell in di station, an dem beat im wid dem batons, dem kick and punch im to. Dem nebba seh dat, but dat's how im get blak an blue. Di policemen bite, bite up dem han an body an seh har son Mark bite dem. Dat is wha dem always do, an di police doctors write de same ting fi support dem."

"Dis a wha dem do to all blak people wen dem ketch dem. Dem hate wi so much dat wen dem get a chance, dem tek out all di white people's hatred in dis country pon wi."

"So wha mek dem nuh tek im a hospital ef im sick," inquired a sobbing mother.

"After dem kick, an beat di daylight outta im, dem lef him eena di cell all night. Next, mawnin dem fine im dead."

The women screamed in pain.

"Im dead jus like dat, nobody nuh jus dead like dat. Dem do im sinting. Dem musa beat im eena im hed, an im hemmoridge," said nurse Annette.

"Poor Sister Sally, mi caan understand how she feels. She bring har pickney yah fi better imself, an di police dem kill im fah no reason. Im nuh did a tief anyting. Im no kill no-one, im a just walk by im self. Im a go bout im business an dem stop im, fi search im an den kill im."

"A wha im coulda seh, fi mek dem react so brutal to im. A more a dem dan im. So why two or three a dem no hold im, an put im eena di van like a human being."

"Dem no tink wi a human being. Yuh nuh si how dem treat wi a work,"

"Di police dem a show wi wha dem a go do wid wi, ef wi no jump an bow low to dem wen dem seh so. Dem a tell wi slave days nuh dun yet. Dem a hab fun wid wi, jus like eena slave days. Eena dem days, ef di Backra waan fi beat yuh til im kill yuh, im coulda dweet an nutten happen to im. Now, di police are di slave master's overseers mi seh, yuh nuh si dat. Lawd, Lawd, dis country wicked nuh. Dem invite us yah fi work, den dem treat wi bad. Den dem kill wi pickney an get way wid it. Dis nuh different from wen wi fore-parents were slaves. Dem seh dem so civilised in dis country now, an dem have laws fi protect di people dem."

"Di law nuh apply to wi, wi blak. blak people nuh hab nuh rights eena dis yah country. All dem waan wi fi do is dem dutty wuk fah nutten. 'Mi nah stay eena dis yah country. Mi cum fah five years an mi nah stay longer dan mi haffi. Mi fraid fah mi pickney dem, especially fah mi boy pickney dem. Dem life no wut nutten eena dis country."

"Dis is di end fah wi an wi bwoy pickney dem. Once yuh si dem get way wid it; di police nah stop. A lot a wi pickney dem gwine ded eena police station in di future. Dem hate wi so much, dem wi do anyting fi mek wi fraid a dem."

Aunty Mackie rallied the women in their hour of pain and grief for their Sister Sally.

"Mi gwine sit wid har tonight. Who a come wid mi? Mi waan fi tek har someting, so mi want fi collect a lickle money fah har. She cyan go a wuk til dis finish. An she nuh hab plenty fambly here fi help har. Wi all haffi help har," she said with a sigh.

The women agreed. They all had boy children at home, and they trembled as they imaged what was awaiting them around every corner. The police vans across the capital and the country were waiting to search their sons under the legitimate 'Stop and Search Laws'. They were also using this law, to lawfully beat and manhandled their boy children and menfolk. Slavery had legally given the overseers and enslavers the right to beat Africans to death without any redress. Nothing had changed in the intervening four hundred and odd years. The police were doing the same thing in the United Kingdom, and as time would show, it would become the trademark of the British police force in their relations with black people, and especially with black youth and men. The more things appeared to change, the more it had remained the same. The time and the circumstances were different, but the results were still the same.

Suddenly, the stories their menfolk had been telling them flooded into their consciousness. Finally, they understood. They reflected and felt guilty, that they had not listened to the stories about the harassment their male children endured, daily at the hands of the police. They vowed to pay attention and act. They would warn their sons and spouses to be cautious of the police. They would tell them to come straight home from school or work. Then, the police would have no reason to stop and search them. They would ask them to walk with a companion. They delved into their pockets and purses and gave generously for Sister Sally. They knew that tomorrow they would be in Sister Sally's shoes.

CHAPTER 19

Saying Goodbye

Aunty Mackie's cramped house in the row of picture painted houses became the centre of the community's funeral preparations. Sister Sally was in the depths of despair because of the murder of her only child by the police. She was locked away in Springfield mental hospital in Tooting. She had busied herself with the preparations for the burial of her only child. Frantically, she had gone to the hospital to see her son but was not allowed to see his body. The mother had asked why she could not see him. She was ushered out with all kinds of excuses, a post-mortem had to be held, then an inquest had to be done. There would be an enquiry after which the body would be released. The boy's mother imagined the unimaginable pain her son had suffered as he was beaten, kicked and sat on by those brutal and obese white policemen. She saw his bruised and disfigured skull. She visualised his smooth Ebony skin and his ashen features, as the blood had drained from his veins onto the cold hard floor.

The mother saw him crying for her in the police van, and again pictured him lying on the floor of the dingy police cell on the dirty, rough floor. It wrenched at her insides. She fell onto her bedroom floor, landing on it as if she was being beaten by the vicious policemen, who had taken the precious life of her young child. She thumped the floor furiously until all feelings drained from her body, as she lay lifeless on the cold linoleum. In her lifelessness, she found her son. The boy hugged and held her firmly, she comforted him, and he assured her that everything was OK. Were they not together now?

The woman stroked her son's knotty black hair, his soft black cheeks and kissed them affectionately, but he withdrew his head as if to say I'm much too old for this sort of thing now. The mother understood, much later she called out to him to bring her some water, and promptly he did. She drank it, and the boy sat at her feet watching the television. Then she heard his bedroom door close, and she called out to him good night. She listened to his muffled response, and rose and went to her room, she would see him in the morning.

Aunty Mackie and the women had found her that evening when they came to help her with the funeral arrangements. The women were frightened that she was dead, they called the ambulance, it took her to hospital. The distressed mother screamed and hollered for her dead son, so she was sent to Springfield Mental Hospital to be assessed. The community rallied around their sister, it was their funeral too. They prepared the funeral, it was a rehearsal for what was awaiting all of them. The mothers with young men in their families waited for the inevitable knock on their front doors. They could only avoid 'the knock' if they died, or left this inhospitable land with their sons and menfolk, a country where their lives and feelings seemed to be of no value to the sadistic proxies, of their reluctant hosts.

"Today we are gathered here to mourn the loss of our young son, Mark. Mark's life was cut short for no good reason that we know of. His encounter with the police on one of their stop and search missions ended his very short life. It is a daily occurrence and a crime against our community and humanity. Daily, no hourly, the youths tell us stories of their encounters with the state's police force. For too long we have ignored their complaints, look, how it has taken a young and productive life from our community," lamented Pastor Andrews.

"Today, we are here to celebrate, rejoice and thank God for our son Mark's short but tragic life. It may seem disrespectful to talk about something, that does not appear to directly relate to our celebration of Mark's short life. Mark's horrific death was avoidable, and it has given us the opportunity to reflect on our situation in this country, so far. However, I can assure you that what I am about to say, is intricately linked to our celebration of Mark's short life. My purpose will become clear as I go along," he told the grieving congregation.

"Every day, our children reveal to us the many problems they face in their schools, we must listen to them. Our sons and daughters have not died violently in schools yet, but the education system destroys them mentally. This happens because the schools our children attend, do not have any expectations of them, they do not believe that they can achieve the highest levels. The school system does not want them to succeed for many reasons, and we know what they are. We brought our children here to be educated because we know we are talented, and that they too are capable of learning and succeeding at all levels.

Our learning goals were destroyed first by slavery, which forbade anyone to teach us to read and write. After our liberation, the colonial government washed its hands of us. Therefore, we had to rely on ourselves and charities for our schooling. In effect, they refused to give us the most basic education. We have provided for ourselves the level of education we have today. In the future, this situation will not change significantly."

"We are invited workers, we were asked to come and help to rebuild this country along with Irish labourers and other Commonwealth citizens, after the destruction of World War II. We accepted the challenge, because it fitted in with our burning desire to shake off our past, and become the people we were born and wanted to be. We migrated for a reason. We accepted the invitation to come and work here, to give our children the opportunities we did not have, and to rise above the perception this society, and its people have of us as cheap low skilled labour."

He stopped, then continued.

"So far, the community and our children's experience of the school system has not been what we wanted and expected. It is as if they are saying to us yet again, as they did during slavery we are forbidding you to learn to read and write. Today, even though you have placed your children in our schools and care, it is not our job to teach them and make them successful members of society. It is your responsibility solely, so get on with it, teach them. If not, we will expel them from our schools onto the streets, where the police and our expanding prisons will gladly take care of them," he emphasised.

"We have listened and understood, we have risen to the challenge, and have set up and are setting up Saturday schools across the country, to give our children the quality schooling the state schools refuse to give them. The Saturday school in Clapham is just one of them, and there are many more where our communities reside. We must sit with our offspring and teach them what we know. We must do as the old people did in the islands, they sat with us, their children and their neighbour's children and made us do our school work. We must make time for our children's education. Our busy and hectic working life is no excuse for not making sure our youths, work inside and outside their schools," the pastor told them.

"We must take education for ourselves and our children. Every parent or guardian in our community must be the person that maps out, guides and controls their children's schooling and education from the moment they learn to talk and enter the school system. It will not be given to us as a right," the vicar stressed.

"How does the celebration of Mark's life link with schooling? Well if we do not prepare our children to the highest levels, they will end up on the streets jobless, and easy targets for the police to stop and search them, and many will die in police cells up and down the country. The courts will send those who survive police brutality to prison for longer periods than they send white youths for the same offences. This system does not want everyone to achieve to the best of their ability and get high-level qualifications. It does not have enough well-paid or rewarding jobs for everyone. The school system will only school a small section of the population to the highest level, and they will get the limited amount of quality jobs and good salaries. These will be the children of those who hold power, and those parents who can pay for their children's schooling in public and private schools," he informed his community.

"And even when we educate ourselves and get reasonable jobs, we will have to work very hard to keep them and be promoted. The education system and the workplaces will use any means necessary to take our jobs from us and throw us onto the scrap heap when it suits them. Those of us without good education or skills will get low-level jobs or no job at all. Many will be forced onto the streets, and the police are paid to deal with us," he told them again.

"Look, our beloved son Mark had a job, but the police stopped and searched him, they found nothing on him, but it resulted in his death. We must make the links and understand the society that we live in now. There are enough prisons to take those of us, who fail in the school system and end up on the streets, or those who challenge their despicable treatment of us. Look how many of our sons and daughters are in prisons and mental institutions already, our numbers are extremely high when compared to the white population, in these institutions," he told his audience.

Pastor Andrews continued.

"Again, I say we must listen to everyone in our community. We must think about and understand everyone's daily experience. We must not continue to only blame individuals for the shortcomings of this society. The society is the problem in most cases, because of its beliefs about us."

Passionately, he carried on.

"We left the islands as invited workers to rebuild this country after World War II. Willingly, we came from nearly all the islands of the Caribbean, and the South American mainland, from the small and big islands. We left Antigua, Barbados Trinidad, French Guiana, Guyana, St Vincent, St Lucia, St Kitts and many more islands to find work and improve the quality of our lives. We have put up with the hardships and have not complained."

"We have had to find ways around the intractable problems of the schooling of our children, in housing, in the workplace, in the social sphere and now our community faces the power of the state, in the form of the police. We have seen our young men killed on the streets by white youths and racist organisations that say that 'Britain must be kept 'white'."

"We must honour those who have died in our community, at the hands of thugs and hooligans including the police."

"The men and women in our community who faced the white mobs and attackers, and have stood their ground, have made it possible for us to walk the streets in relative safety now. We are not over the hill yet. The white thugs and their organisations have not finished with us yet. They are waiting to attack us yet again if they think we are napping and when the opportunity arises, and when the way is cleared for them by those in authority, and the police force," he said.

"We must be diligent and always defend each other. An attack on one is an attack on all of us. We put ourselves and our community, in the greatest conceivable danger if we do not stand together, against the racist threat from all thugs and the state to our lives and limbs."

"What has this to do with Mark's death? Well, everything. Mark died because he was alone, and we had not put in place or understood fully the threat facing our community, from all sections of this society. By understanding the threat that faces every one of us, and becoming our brother and sister's keeper, we may not have to bury more of our young men. Does the scripture not tell us to be our sister and brothers' keeper? Why haven't we followed this teaching? Our community will continue to pay significantly, if we do not listen and heed the words of the Lord, God our Father in heaven. All of us must be our brother and sister's keeper from now on."

He stopped and looked intently at the congregation, and then said, "Let's sing Martin Luther's rallying cry 'We shall overcome'". We need to, so they rose, and the words of the song penetrated deep into their souls. Their harmonious noise filled the in and outside of the small Methodist Church and spilt out onto the noisy traffic filled main road. They were singing because of the slaying of their young son Mark, by the police. They were also singing for the multitudes before them, who had been murdered and ill-treated purely because of the colour of their skin. They were singing too, for all those young men who would be killed in one form or other by the British police force in the years to come, they were attempting to come to terms with their pain and grief.

In the words of the songs that the congregation sang, the agony and sorrow of their migration experiences were acknowledged. They were echoing the deep pain and heartache, that their brothers and sisters, along with the Africans in 'The Enslaved World', had lived and had to confront before them.

We shall overcome they chanted, over and over until they felt some relief from their intense pain and sorrow. The Pastor started, and the congregation followed solemnly and knowingly, "Our Father which art in heaven'.

When the prayer finished, they acknowledged the sentiments in unity.

"Amen, Amen, Amen," they bawled.

Then the hairdresser spoke.

"Wen Sister Sally walk through di front door of mi lickle house in Poplar Road, one cold an freezing winter's day, she bring young Mark wid har. Mark was a good bwoy pickney, raised by im grannie in Trinidad, in di old-time way," the hairdresser stressed.

"She teach im manners, she learn im fi look afta imself."

"Im nebba pass big people an nuh seh 'good morning' or 'good day'."

"Im respectful."

"Eena di holiday Sister Sally lef im wid mi an mi sister, wi nuh hab nuh trouble wid im. Im go a shop fah wi, im bring back wi change. Im do im school work, wi nuh haffi tell him nutten. Mark was di son mi always wanted, im was fi mi pickney to. Di police kill im dead fah no reason. Wen dem kill him, dem kill im mother an mi to. Dem kill all a wi dat day."

"Today wi here in church fi celebrate Mark's life. Im a all a wi son an pickney. Wi haffi remember im is jus di latest one eena wi community dat dem killed. An wi haffi talk out at times like dese, so wi all undastan wha a gwaan, so wi caan all do someting bout it."

"From di time wi set foot eena dis yah country wi haffi live in fear, because many white people nuh like wi because wi skin black. Teddy boys beat up wi boys and men eena di streets. Dem kill Kelso Cochrane in West London soon afta im cum yah. Dem beat up some a wi eena Notting Hill, an all oba London an di countryside. 'In Nottingham, wey a lot of blak people settle, di Teddy Boys attack dem, dem haffi defend dem selves. Wi haffi fight back or else dem wooda kill all a wi. Wi did lucky fi hab dem ex-service men wid training from World War One an Two, a dem organise wi fi stop di thugs an dem leader dat waan fi kill all a wi. Ef wi nebba fight back wen di thugs attack wi, dem wooda still be afta wi. Di police do nutten fi stop dem, dem in league wid dem.' Di white people doan waan wi eena dem pubs, dem houses, dem hotels, dem clubs, dem churches, dem social organisations, an dem country an wi all know dis. So wi lef eena, wi houses an di street.

So, di people fram Trinidad organise dem lickle carnival eena Notting Hill. Dem dweet fah wi fi enjoy wi self an forget fah a moment di awfulness of dis country, an di people. Mi hear seh it was a ooman fram Trinidad called Claudia Jones dat start di lickle carnival, an she had a newspaper to. So wha dem do? Dem come an bruk it up. Wi nuh fi do nutten. All wi fi do is wuk night an day fah di lickle money, an stay eena wi cold and damp houses an rooms. Blak people cyan feel safe yah. Look, now di police tek oba an a lawfully kill wi an wi pickney dem."

"Di police raid any lickle place wi hab, dem seh dem a look fah drugs. Dem raid wi get-togethers an seh wi sell drinks an it illegal an nizey. Dem try fi lock wi up. Wen wi try an set up a lickle business dem interfere an talk bout di law. Dem try fi stop wi running a lickle enterprise fi improve wi self. A dat wi come yah fi do nuh? Dem raid Brother Critchlow's restaurant eena Notting Hill. Wi nuh fi have nuh wey fi meet, an tek di pressures dat dem place squarely pon wi shoulders ebery day. Dem arres im an t'row im eena prison fah months, fi mek im business mash-up. But wi haffi tank dem people like Brother Critchlow because ef it nuh fah dem wi wooda nuh hab nuh business place in dis country today. Dem blaze di trail fah wi. And dere is many more blak people like Brother Critchlow, who stan up an fight so wi couda come afta dem. An wen dem arres Brother Critchlow, wi people did go a im restaurant fi support him, and di police arres dem to, and charge dem wid all kinda foolishness."

"Dem charge man an woman, and tek dem a court and tink dat dem a go accept it. But dem defend dem selves, one a dem fram di same island as Aunt Sally, im a study fi be a lawyer, so dem nebba know, so im defend imself an win all a dem big time white lawyers eena di court. Im name Darcus Howe, im come fram Trinidad to. Mi seh eena di early days di people fram Trinidad do a lot a tings fah wi, dem did organise good."

"Brother Critchlow was a tinking man. Im use di money im get fram im brothers an sisters to put back someting eena di blak community. Im set up a community centre fah blak people oba West London an all oba London. Fram dat day forward wi hab a place fi meet, get information bout wi rights an relax. Tank him Lawd, tank him."

"Mi haffi seh dis cause it a truu. Di blak community nuh waan people dat a go hands an glove up, wid white people. An grin wid dem an dem organisations an tink dat, dat a go help blak people eena di long run.' Mi seh wi community nuh need dem blak individuals who side wid di white people an do dem dutty work gainst wi. Dem kick dung dem own fah di white people fi get a lickle promotion. Dem use wi own people gainst wi ebery day. Di divide an rule tactic of di white people is as old as time wi know dat, so whe wi nuh stik together. A ongle wi a go lose wen dem divide and rule wi."

"Wi waan blak people who wi stan up to dem, like Claudia Jones, Brother Critchlow an di bredas and sistas dat did support im wen dem arres im, like Darcus Howe, Althea Lecointe, Godfrey Millette, Barbara Beese, Rupert Boyce, Rothwell Kentish and Rhodan Gordon. A dem people wi need aroun wi ebery day, wid dem wi will go forwaad as a community and people."

"Di white man only respects dem dat lick him an stan up to im. Wi haffi stan up to im, all a wi together. Mi gwine seh dis fah Mark. Mi a seh dis fah all di policeman dem, di judges an di politicians; wi nah accept dis yah brutality and murder of wi youth. Wi nah stand fah it. It dun now, it stop now, or as oonu seh eena di Queen's English."

"We have had enough; we are not standing for any more of this," she said defiantly.

"Di blak community nuh wan nuh more a it," she stressed finally.

Loudly, the congregation agreed. Mark's death had given them the opportunity to vent their anger and frustration on the society that had asked them to come and rebuild the mother country. But instead of treating them as wanted guests, and equal citizens they had treated them atrociously. They had been hostile and reluctant hosts.

"Our blessed son Mark will go to his father and our father in heaven. Praise the Lord, glorify our Father in heaven, blessed is thy name. May your Kingdom come to this heathen land, where the colour of a young man's skin gives the police the right to kill him legally. You know our Lord what we face in this country, we know that you will give us the strength to work together to overcome it."

"Ashes to ashes dust to dust as we put our beloved son Mark into the ground and into your hands our Lord Jesus Christ," stated Pastor Andrews

"Amen, Amen, Amen, Amen," wailed the congregation.

Sister Sally screamed in agony as the body of her innocent, young and beautiful son was finally taken from her and placed into the cold and freezing earth. The church and congregation were with her. They allowed her time with her only son before his body would be covered and she would be left alone with only her memories.

"Mi mada, an mi Lawd God look afta im fah mi nuh, mi cyan dweet nuh more," she bawled.

Then she sank into the cold, bitter earth.

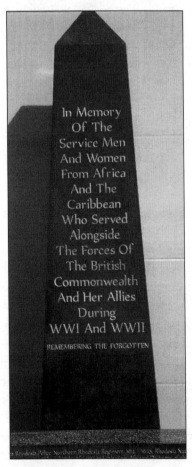

Memorial to African and Caribbean volunteer soldiers in WW1 and WW11
Photo: B. Ellis

CHAPTER 20

Reflections

Brothers and sisters, the islanders and the mainlanders, have told us about their welcome and some of their experiences in the United Kingdom after 22nd June 1948, a hundred and ten years after their ancestors' emancipation in August 1838. Were there any signs of change on the part of the nation that had enslaved their forebears, to make amends for their past actions? Were they welcomed and appreciated for their contribution to Britain and her allies' victory during World War I and II, as well as their contribution to the rebuilding of Britain at the end of World War II? These very motivated, ambitious and hard-working migrants, could not have predicted the response to their arrival and treatment in the country, that they were schooled to believe was the mother country, as they prepared to leave the Americas.

I, Anancy, Ananse will argue that the 15th Century colonising agenda of the European nations continued to shape the relationship, between the immigrants and their hosts, in the United Kingdom more than four hundred years later. I sincerely believe that the Windrush generation's experiences and their response to them, in the United Kingdom was a continuation of the liberation struggle waged by their fore-parents, who liberated themselves from slavery, in 1838. Any modifications to the colonial agenda, however, reflected the changing conditions in 20th Century Britain and their tenacious resistance to their continued economic, social and institutionalised repression after 1948, you may disagree.

Therefore, we must focus on their enormous contribution to changes in the United Kingdom and in their own circumstances after 1948, despite the hurdles they faced arising from a social and economic system; that worked principally to maintain the interests and power of many of the descendants of the former enslavers. Naturally, the successes of the Windrush generation and their children in the United Kingdom are prolific. It goes without saying, that they and their children must write into world history, their contributions and achievements because white British society and those who write history textbooks and academic papers will not be so generous.

The Windrush generation and their children changed the United Kingdom because they were determined to improve the quality of life for themselves, their children and their communities. They intended to transform the islands and the mainland of the Americas so that they could return one day. They enhanced the quality of life for the citizens of the United Kingdom and must take credit for playing their part in creating the multiracial and multicultural society, that exists today. They did so by helping the indigenous white population to be tolerant of migrants daily, they enabled them to co-exist with immigrants in their workplaces, in schools, churches and the rest of society.

The first task of the Windrush generation was to secure the streets of Britain for their community and other immigrants from the fascist thugs led by Oswald Mosley in London, Nottingham and many other cities. Mosley and his mobs had threatened them because they were against immigration. They wanted non-white people returned to their countries of origin, and an end to migration to Britain and Europe. They wanted to keep Britain and Europe white. The second task, of the children born to the Windrush generation and raised in the United Kingdom, was to challenge the inequalities which denied them a decent education, jobs, housing and the right to walk the streets of Britain without excessive harassment by the state's police force. The police force was lawfully using Section 4 of The Vagrancy Act 1824, 'to stop and search individuals they suspected of loitering to commit an arrestable offence', black British youths became their principal target. Therefore, I believe that the second generation reopened the debate on inequality in British society, for themselves, the white working classes and for all citizens of the United Kingdom. The Windrush generation and their children constantly challenged the historical role allocated to them as a low-wage workforce and 'second-class citizens'.

One of the most significant contributions of the Windrush generation, from 1948 onwards, I think, was to reopen and challenge the British school system's deep-rooted belief and practice, that only a small section of the school population could learn and achieve to the highest levels. The incoming migrants were not encouraged and recruited into the sought-after professions, as teachers, doctors, lawyers, journalists, university teaching staff, trade union officials, the police force, captains of industry and multi-national companies. However, they and their children were determined to move into these professions naturally. Many had to redo their island and mainland qualifications to get British certification, then fight to overcome the prejudice and discrimination within these occupations and in their workplaces. They would put an end to the society's deep-seated conviction that they were only suited to manual labour.

Marcus Mosiah Garvey died in Britain on 10th June 1940, eight years before the Windrush docked at Tilbury after being deported from the United States of America. He would have predicted their reception and subsequent experiences in the United Kingdom, after 1948; not because he had lived in Britain for many years or was able to see into the future. He was able to do this because he understood how the international monetary and legal systems worked, to benefit only a small section of the population in each country.

In the 1920s and 1930s, Marcus Garvey had told Africans in the Americas and Africa to "Stand up ye Mighty Race," a rallying cry for them to take control of their economic future and destiny. He had said this because the financial and social system in the past had not met the needs of Africa and its Diaspora because it had not been created for them. The economic system was designed to exploit them, and the mass of the world's population and it would continue to do so, in the future. He had encouraged and directed the organisations of the African Diaspora, to set up their own financial and social systems, to improve their lives, because the present-day commercial, industrial, financial and social networks, would not meet their need for economic independence, social mobility and human dignity.

Initially, the Windrush's generation was not welcomed into the teaching profession or the police force, even though students who met the requirements were trained in British institutions as teachers in the colonies. However, their children entered these revolving door occupations naturally with British qualifications. Local Education and Police Authorities advertised and recruited black teachers, policemen and women, decades after decades yet their numbers did not rise and stabilise significantly. Many recruits in both professions left in higher numbers, than their white colleagues because of the racist attitudes and practices in their workplaces, which prevented them from progressing naturally into leadership positions.

The police and the teaching profession have used and continue to use some of the most discriminatory and unethical practices against the Black and Ethnic minority staff in their ranks, the case of PC Howard versus the Metropolitan Police in 2014 is a good example. In the teaching profession, there are many recorded cases of head teachers using discriminatory and unlawful procedures against newly qualified and established Black and Minority Ethnic teachers with the support of their governing bodies, unions and local education authorities. Retaining Black and Ethnic minority workers have never been at the centre of the recruitment strategies of these and other professions. The rapidly changing ideologies of the two political parties further reinforced the revolving door policies and practices towards the islanders and their children in both careers.

Racism had not diminished, disintegrated, disappeared or died in the United Kingdom with the older generation of white working-class people; that the Race Relation Industry of the 1970s and 80s had said were the perpetrators of racism in the United Kingdom. To be fair, many white working-class people had no option but to get along with the incoming islanders, mainlanders and the Asian population or move out to the suburbs. Many of the white working-class who remained in the inner cities lived and worked alongside immigrants, and over time they became good neighbours and colleagues in workplaces supporting each other in troubled times until their retirement. In their old age, many of the white population were cared for by the immigrants that came after 1948. Their lives became interconnected, and they tolerated each other.

However, time had not erased racism from British institutions and the younger generation as the 21st Century commenced, even with the ageing 1965 and 1976 Race Relation Acts respectively, and subsequent legislation which the immigrant community organisations had pushed governments to implement. Both **Acts** were passed by the United Kingdom's Parliament to prevent discrimination on the grounds of **race**. Despite the Acts and subsequent revisions of the legislation, many young middle-class people moving into the inner cities for cheaper housing and employment did not want to live alongside immigrants and their children. They intended to create middle class enclaves in the inner cities. They wanted white middle-class neighbours and schools for their children, they were determined to push out the remaining British born blacks and their families from these localities.

The Rampton Report 1981, completed by the Swann Report 1985, inquired into the schooling of black children, the Macpherson Report 1999 investigated policing. The police's investigation of the murder of Stephen Lawrence by young racist white thugs in 1993. The 1999 report stated that "institutional racism' was and is a key factor in the police force and its investigation of Stephen Lawrence's murder. The Swann Report concluded that institutional racism prevented Black and Ethnic Minority learners from reaching their full potential in the school system. It could also be argued that this also applies to many black professionals in most occupations. In October 2017, the Prime Minister, Theresa May vowed to tackle racism, after a report, she commissioned revealed the shocking extent of discrimination in the United Kingdom, she admitted that the Black and Minority Ethnic communities already knew the magnitude of inequality and racism in British society. The Windrush generation and their children had continuously challenged the established view and explanations of governments and some institutions that racism was a phenomenon practised by individuals and a particular social class. They forced the state and its institutions to acknowledge racism and discrimination as an institutional and structural component of British society and its system of government with its origins in the justification of the slave trade and slavery.

The laws enacted by the two Race Relations Acts was implemented by the Councils for Racial Equality in each borough. In the early days, they were responsible for promoting the rights of the immigrant communities, combating racism and discrimination and promoting tolerance. Ansel Wong was Principal Race Equality Adviser to the London Strategic Policy Unit and was previously Senior Race Relations Adviser to the Greater London Council. He established a community education centre in Paddington and pioneered one of the first black supplementary schools in Britain. He co-authored with Addai-Sebo in 2017, the Black History Month Magazine which recorded and celebrated the thirtieth year of this annual event in the United Kingdom.

Herman Ouseley was appointed as the first principal race relations advisor in local government and served as Head of the GLC's Ethnic Minority Unit. He later became Chief Executive of the London Borough of Lambeth and the former Inner London Education Authority (the first black person to hold such an office). He was responsible for over 1000 schools and colleges across London. In 1993, he became the executive chairman of the Commission for Racial Equality, a position he held until 2000. He worked extensively in the community and in the race relation industry. Mr Ouseley is now Lord Ouseley and is a member of the House of Lords.

Trevor Phillips was born in London of Caribbean parents in 1953, he studied at Imperial College London, and was elected President of the National Union of Students in 1978. He is a writer and former TV journalist. Mr Phillips co-authored with Mike Phillips 'Windrush: The Irresistible Rise of Multi-Racial Britain' on the fiftieth anniversary of the Windrush. He was chairman of the Runnymede Trust which promotes Racial Equality and was head of the Commission for Racial Equality from 2003 to 2006. He chaired the Equality and Human Rights Commission from 2006. He was made an Officer of the Order of the British Empire in 1999.

Exposed daily to the injustices of the education system and society, this very determined community set up their own Saturday schools, these school did what mainstream schools had failed to do, they began to prepare the pupils for educational success and social mobility. The Abeng Centre in Brixton, now called the Karibu

Education Centre was set up by the Reverend Tony Ottey in the 1970s to provide a supplementary school and a centre for the community and the youth. It still serves them in the 21st century. Today, after-school and Saturday learning provisions are abundant on Britain's High Streets and community organisations under different names and guises. The Windrush generation pioneered supplementary schooling services in the United Kingdom, for all parents if they need and want to use them.

The migrants and their children greatly enhanced the profits of British industry, and the fledgeling nationalised services and industries from their arrival. These included the railways and buses, the Post Office, and especially the National Health Service. They worked very long and unsociable hours for minimum pay, very limited or no promotion to responsible and higher paid jobs in their workplaces. Their role in the National Health Service as nurses, midwives, matrons, cleaners, porters and auxiliaries are well documented. Their contribution strengthened the newly formed health service from its infancy, in 1948 to adulthood to become a robust and mature service which many communities defend today. However, some of these experienced health professionals also succumbed to the revolving door policies of governments and the administration of the National Health Service. Subsequently, some left the service, when nursing services were restructured as an all degree profession some years ago, with priority entrance and promotion going mainly to young white graduates. However, they and their children returned to the National Health Service and were boosted by workers from Africa, the Philippines and many other third world countries when the white health professionals moved on to more prestigious jobs.

Similarly, island and mainland workers manned the railways, the underground and the buses. The 150th anniversary of London Transport acknowledged their contribution from the 1950s. It highlighted the continuity in the recruitment process which started in the islands, as the children of the first recruits, joined their parents in this sector, this was what society expected them to do. Many of their children later suffered from the privatisation and reorganisation of the railways and the transport services by successive governments.

This resulted in drastic changes in the management structure, which favoured white staff to the exclusion of these experienced workers and their children. The islanders, especially the young women returned to these services when the bus and rail companies were short staffed and in crisis.

Annually, the island's women in the railway industry were crowned as 'canteen queens'. The women also made, served tea and swept and scrubbed the floors of Lyon's tearooms in London's West End, after their arrival. If the jobs were low status and low paid, and the white population did not want them, they were welcome to them. They would have to wait until the prestigious and gainful occupations were in decline, then they would be recruited to staff them, services that had seen better days. The relatively well-paid garbage collection service of the 70s and 80s is a good example. It was a closed shop mainly staffed by white working- class men. In the 21st Century, of minimum wage and zero hours contracts, it is now a low paid and contracting service that is staffed by the white working class and immigrants from all over the world.

While the British press and institutions praised the Windrush generation for their hard work and dedication in carrying out low-status jobs meticulously; the same newspapers depicted their British-born children, especially the young men as thieves, muggers and criminals. In general, the British press created and perpetuated negative images of immigrant communities, after 1948. The black Media in Britain was the response to the negative portrayal of the black community, especially of black British youths. Marcus Garvey and Claudia Jones had developed newspapers that had local and global circulation. Claudia Jones was born in Trinidad but went to live in the United States of America in 1955, later she came to Britain because of her political activities. These journals and publications gave an African or black perspective on many issues, and they also organised and informed the community of their rights, as well as maintaining the links with their homelands.

The well-known and well used black newspapers in the early days told the stories the white press refused to write, they opposed the negative images the white media circulated about the community and their children. They wrote positive stories with constructive descriptions of black youth and the community's contribution to British society. Publications such as the *West Indian Gazette, Afro-Asian Caribbean News, West Indian World, Caribbean Times, The Voice* and the *Jamaica Gleaner* informed, campaigned and built support around the problematic issues the community faced, such as the SUS laws. Community groups also organised and published their own journals and broadsheets about local issues in their communities.

The Race Today Collective based in Brixton and coordinated by Darcus Howe concentrated on the many national and international problems faced by the black and Asian communities, they explained and focused on schooling, the community's experience of the police and the criminal justice system, in the early years. The *Race & Class* journal founded by Ambalavaner Sivanandan provided a scholarly response to the issues faced by immigrant communities in the United Kingdom and the world over the last thirty years. The publication's central themes were and are racism, empire and globalisation and the impact on world communities.

Professor Stuart Hall like Ambalavaner Sivanandan focused on race and class issues in the United Kingdom and internationally. Professor Hall was an islander who arrived in England in 1951 to study. At the end of his studies at Oxford University, his writing challenged the long-established view of social class in British society, and especially the representation of immigrants after 1948. He developed with colleagues the 'Cultural Studies' genre which explained and questioned the structure of British society and its institutions' effect on different social groups in the population. It became one of the models used in universities for research and academic study. Professor Hall was committed to showing the positive contributions of black and white working-class people to British society throughout history. In Birmingham, he supported many scholars from the island and the mainland community to write about and analyse Britain's past and present relationship with her ex-colonies, the immigrant communities, black youths and the education system's response to the children of the post-war immigrants. He maintained that the island communities were in Britain because the British had colonised their homelands.

The evolving black press in Britain gave the children of the Windrush generation, the opportunity to practise the skills they had studied for because, in the early days, it was rare for black journalists to be employed by British newspapers or television companies. It helped them to get the skills and confidence to pursue careers in journalism in the years to come.

It goes without saying, that the immigrant communities were not represented in the United Kingdom's publishing houses, although the community had a lot to say about their experiences in Britain. Community publishers, such as New Beacon Books, Bogle L'Ouverture Press, Hansib Publications, Karia Press, Tamarind Books, Xpress and later BIS publications gave the islands and mainland's writers a voice, as well as providing for those who had something to say with the support and an opening to express themselves. Verna Wilkins set up Tamarind Books, to offer young black, children positive self-images. Ama Gueye's annual Black Dolls Expo gave children and parents the opportunity to physically see and handle a range of black dolls, and images made by members of the community for sale. Their racial and cultural identity were being celebrated and reinforced in the United Kingdom.

The publishing houses promoted and distributed work by black writers who were often rejected by white mainstream publishers because they chose to write about issues that affected their communities. These issues were often ignored and seen as unimportant by the publishing houses and the British press. These bookshops held book fairs, linked and distributed the writings of Africa and its Diaspora. But most importantly they helped to record the Windrush generation and their children's history. They also created job opportunities and learning spaces for them and their children, and have become role models for future generations.

The literacy campaigns of the 1970s and 80s, also gave immigrants from the islands and the mainland and the Commonwealth countries a voice. They taught immigrants the English language as well as learning to read and write, for those who had missed out on their earlier schooling, in the United Kingdom and Commonwealth countries. The students talked and were helped to write about their experiences in Britain and their homelands. Their reminiscences were recorded in small booklets. Some of these literacy provisions were in bookshops. They were The Bookplace in Peckham, Deptford Bookshop, Centerprise in Stoke Newington, Soma Books in Kennington, the North Kensington Community and Cambridge House projects in Camberwell, as well as many other literacy projects and bookshops in the United Kingdom.

Linton Kwesi Johnson joined his mother in England in 1963; his poetry voiced the anger of alienated black youth at the time. His poem 'Sonny's Lettah' summed up the experiences and frustration of young black men and women from the 1970s onwards with the police and society. The young people were frustrated with the racism and discrimination they experienced daily, at all levels of British society and especially at the hands of the police in the inner cities. Heavy-handed policing in the inner cities resulted in riots in Bristol in 1980 and 1981; in Moss Side in Manchester; Handsworth in Birmingham; Brixton in London; and Toxteth in Liverpool. Four years later, the Brixton and Broadwater Farm riots were triggered by the shooting of 'Cherry' Groce by the police at her home in Brixton. A few months later, Cynthia Jarrett died from heart failure after the police raided her home on Broadwater Farm. In 2014, the Metropolitan Police Commissioner apologised "unreservedly" for the shooting and the time it had taken to say "sorry" following an inquest into the death of Dorothy 'Cherry' Groce. The community and their children had put pressure on the police force to acknowledge their discriminatory and brutal policing in immigrant communities.

At the same time, historians of the Windrush generation and their children began writing and rewriting literature and history to reflect schools, society, their experiences and to record their community's struggles and successes. Some of our ground-breaking historians are Stephen Bourne, Mike and Trevor Phillips, Morgan Dalphinis, Joan Amin-Addo, Robin Walker, Andrea Levy, Margaret Busby, Ismahil Blagrove, Ziggi Alexander, Audrey Dewjee, Paul Crooks and Paul Gilroy.

The island and mainland literary stars wrote for their community and society, they created positive images and reflected the experiences of their generation. They are Samuel Selvon, Andrew Salkey, James

Berry, Beryl Gilroy, Petronella Breingburg, Trish Cooke, Sandra Agard, Mallorie Blackman, Children's Laureate 2013-2015. Benjamin Zephaniah, Floella Benjamin, John Agard, Grace Nicols, Valerie Bloom, Accabre Huntley, Everal Mckenzie and many, many more.

On the stage, screen and television, the Windrush generation gave the United Kingdom legendary comedians, actors, radio and television presenters and newsreaders. They are Lennie James, Judith Jacobs, Moira Stewart, Diane Parish, Juilet Alexander, Gary Wilmot, Don Warrington, Rudolph Walker, Nina Baden-Semper, Corrina Skinner-Carter, Carmen Munroe and Mona Hammond. Other notable performers are Richard Blackwood, Lenny Henry, Felix Dexter, Angie Lamar, Norman Beaton, David Harewood, Nikk Amuka-Bird, Adrian Lester, Nicholas Berry, Paul Barber, Wesley Kerr, Trevor McDonald, Clive Myrie, Vincent Herbert, Mark Wadsworth, Ronke Phillips and Trevor Phillips to name a few.

Menelik Shabazz, filmmaker (director of Burning an Illusion, Lover's Rock and Looking for Love) is a son of the Windrush Generation, he came to Britain from Barbados at the age of six. He was one of the first to use film to document the experiences of his generation. He recorded his generation's development in Britain, their struggles and their achievements. His films document the youth's battles with the criminal justice system, e.g. the police and the SUS laws from the 1970s onwards as well as his communities' positive achievements.

Steve McQueen, director of the film Twelve Years A Slave, was born in London of Grenadian and Trinidadian parents, he is definitely a child of the Windrush generation. He was awarded an Oscar for directing Twelve Years A Slave in March 2014. Steve McQueen's experience and his educational journey through school to college and finally to university, personify the experiences of many of the children of the Windrush generation. Steven McQueen rose above the expectation his secondary school had of him and many students from the island and the mainland community, to only do manual work.

Talawa and the Blue Mountain Theatre groups are based in London but perform throughout the United Kingdom and especially in the black community. Their roots are in the Caribbean, and their stage productions reflect this. Both theatres provide a platform for young actors, actress and school students to develop their skills and talents to reach broader audiences in theatre in the United Kingdom. They offer opportunities for the island and the mainland communities to learn about and see the works of Caribbean writers being performed. Talawa was founded by Yvonne Brewster, Carmen Munroe, Mona Hammond and Inigo Espejel, actors who have inspired their community and the young generation. They have become role models for future generations.

The substantial numbers of black art galleries in the United Kingdom, and especially those in London over the last 70 years have always displayed the works of the community's up and coming artists. These galleries have consistently provided spaces for local artists to showcase their work to the public and school students to enjoy and draw inspiration from their work. Many of these painters are not household names. However, their creativity is known in their local communities.

Some of the established groups and individuals in the black art world are Frank Bowling, Sonya Boyce, Eugene Palmer, Janice Sylvia Brock, Donald Rodney, Eddie Chambers, Dominic Dawes, Claudette Johnson, Wenda Leslie, Ian Palmer, Merlene Smith and Keith Piper and community artist Ken McCalla. Many of the black Art group members were children of Caribbean migrants raised in the industrial landscape in and around the West Midlands. Their first exhibition, *Black Art An' Done*, was held at a Wolverhampton Art Gallery and focused on the concerns of the black community and racial prejudice. The group sought to empower black artists in the community and school students to continue to develop and reflect their communities and society through their artwork.

Many self-help groups, individuals and organisations set up support and pressure groups as well as campaigns around a range of issues affecting the community as the years progressed. The West Indian Standing Conference is one of the oldest island and mainland institutions in Britain. It has served and promoted the interests of the African-Caribbean community, for over fifty-seven years. The organisation was set up by Joe Hunt and other community members soon after they arrived in England. The WISC has been instrumental in pressing governments to put in place legislation to combat racism in the United Kingdom and to continually review policies and practice to fight discrimination and racism in all areas of the society. Clarence C. Thompson MBE, the current Chairman of the West Indian Standing Conference, and the WISC campaigned for the creation of Windrush Square in Brixton to commemorate the contribution of the Windrush generation and the ship that brought them seventy years ago.

Arthur Torrington, Sam King and community members set up the Windrush Foundation, to keep alive the memories and achievements of those who arrived on the ship, and subsequent ships and aeroplanes as well as their tremendous impact on and contribution to their community and the development of United Kingdom.

Community organisations, the community and many, many individuals within it, have worked hard to record, remember, celebrate and keep alive the struggles and achievements of their ancestors. The West Indian Association of Service Personnel (WASP) was set up by Jamaican WWII veterans to provide support and comradeship to ex-servicemen and women from the Caribbean. Today, their headquarters in Clapham, London, serves as a meeting place for all the black community.

Jak Beula and the community funded the African and Caribbean War Memorial in memory of those who died in the WWI and II as well as plaques for the African diaspora that have made enormous contributions to the community and British society. The war memorial is situated outside the Black Cultural Archive building in Brixton. The 2007, memorial group was formed in January 2005 by volunteers to erect a permanent monument for the enslaved Africans and their descendants on a site in the Rose Gardens of London's Hyde Park. The memorial statue was designed by leading International Artist Les Johnson. It will be erected with financial support from the community.

Dr Aggrey Burke, Sandwell's African-Caribbean Mental Health Foundation, as well as Black Mental Health UK, have shaped and campaigned for the development of mental health services for islanders, mainlanders and their children in the United Kingdom.

The African-Caribbean Leukaemia Society set up by Orin Lewis, and the Sickle Cell and Thalassaemia Support Group in Barking, Dagenham, founded by Cecilia Shoetan and the community have supported and worked with many community members affected by these physical and mental health issues.

The Society of Black Lawyers, community support groups and organisations have had to represent and campaign against the disproportionate numbers of black men in prisons, in the United Kingdom compared to the white prison population. They have also highlighted the higher sentences given to black offenders by the courts when compared to white inmates. They have informed and campaigned with the community on many legal issues facing young people. Joint Enterprise is the most recent, and multifaceted concerns in the community. It is used by the courts to prosecute young people who are within close proximity to knife crimes resulting in injury or the death.

The Society also took up the case of university lecturers faced with discrimination in their workplace, over many years after their trade union and its officials failed to take up their concerns. Black and Minority Ethnic members made up the highest percentage of trade unionists, much higher than white trade unionists in the United Kingdom in the 1980s and 1990s. They joined trade unions because they bore the brunt of management brutality, as well as ongoing problems with their fellow workers and lack of promotion in their workplaces. Fortunately, for all trade unionists, there were exceptional black and white trade union officers, women and men who did not succumb to pressure from New Labour to promote management's agenda at the expense of their subscription paying members in the workplace from 1997 onwards. They continued to do the job they were being paid to do, to defend their members in workplaces. These committed trade unionists knew from experience and history that management and workers were not equal partners in the workplace as suggested by New Labour's 'New Unionism'. These trade union officers had to work double time in and outside of their workplaces, to make up for the work many of their colleagues did not do because they were supporting business and management's agendas. Some Black and Minority Ethnic women (Tessa) trade union officers and representatives worked very hard to support their members and members of other unions during this period, even though they faced extreme hostility, from New Labour, the trade union hierarchy and the management in their workplaces.

Bill Morris, now Lord Morris of Handsworth, came to Britain in 1954 to join his mother. He joined the Transport and General Workers Union (TGWU) soon after starting work. In 1992, he became the first black General Secretary of the trade union at a time when trade unionism was under threat from the Conservative government. A staunch supporter of trade unionism, Mr Morris worked to improve the working conditions and pay of his members, many of whom were recruited from the Caribbean in the 1950s. In 2003, he retired from the TGWU and was appointed to many committees to improve the conditions of all workers in Britain.

Glenroy Watson has been a trade union activist and representative of The National Union of Rail, Maritime and Transport Union (RMT) formerly the TGWU for many years. He is also Secretary of the Global Afrika Congress UK, which convenes an annual Reparation Conference under the sponsorship of the union he represents the RMT. Mr Watson defended his members from abuse by management in a period when many trade union officers did not deliver the services their subscription paying members were paying them to provide. He has been a candidate for president of the RMT union in the past.

Fortunately, for many islands and mainland employees and trade unionists in the Rail, Maritime and Transport union, their general secretary Bob Crow and the RMT did not abandon them for management during New Labour's 'New Unionism'. The RMT and their leaders often came under attack from the national press, the Conservative Party, business organisations, New Labour leaders and the public for doing the work, their members, paid them to do with their yearly subscriptions, to defend them in the workplace against brutish and incompetent managers and exploitative business practices.

The Association of Black Police Officers was formed because black police officers experienced acute racism and discrimination in and outside their workplaces. The association supported its members to get their grievances heard which also helped the Black and Minority Ethnic communities.

Incredibly, in 2010, the trade union movement became active once again, the threat from the newly elected Conservative and Liberal Democratic government propelled the unions into action. They began in their own words 'to prepare to fight the Conservatives'. The most prominent trade union in the United Kingdom advertised for union representatives, the union replaced its dormant reps with active ones who would now stand up to management. The same managers they had helped to suppress and get rid of their members in workplaces. The General Secretary of the Trade Union Congress was quietly pensioned off and was replaced by a female. Subsequently, those unions that were notorious for not supporting their subscription paying members placed large adverts in newspapers, encouraging workers to join their unions. The author is not aware of any apology made by the unions to their members to date. The islanders, the mainlanders and their children have had to learn valuable and painful lessons about the limitations of the trade union movement in the United Kingdom.

The East London Black Women's Organisation (ELBOW), Brixton Black Women's Group, Southhall Black Sisters, the Organisation of Women of African and Asian Descent (OWAAD), and the Alliance of Afrikan Women organised around issues which affected women in the community. Beverley Bryan, Suzanne Scafe and Stella Dadzie wrote *The Heart of the Race: Black Women's Lives in Britain* which highlighted the issues facing women and the schooling of the community's children, especially the boys. *Schooling Black Children in Britain: A Practical Guide* was an attempt by the author to galvanise parents into taking total control of their children's schooling in 1995 because research continued to show the under attainment of the communities' children.

The Manhood Academy and its founder Davis J Williams has focused on 'Rites of Passage' and support for boys and men. Luton's Black Men's Community Group has concentrated on issues specific to men of African descent and matters affecting those in the island and mainland community in the United Kingdom.

African Liberation Day gatherings throughout the United Kingdom associated with Cecil Gutsmore and many other community members in the United Kingdom, connected the islanders and the mainlanders to Africa's struggles for independence from the colonial regimes in Southern Africa, as well as the trials and tribulations in their adopted home. African Remembrance Day, was founded by brothers Onyekachi and Chidiwere Wambu, to mark the passing of millions of Africans on their way from Africa to the plantations of the Americas from the 15th Century onwards on Emancipation Day 1st August each year.

Every year, on the 1st August, Emancipation Day, Esther Stanford-Xosei, various reparation committees and individuals in the United Kingdom, have organised petitions and marches to demand recognition and an apology for the atrocities carried out against Africa and its Diaspora, from the 15th Century onwards. They have also campaigned for reparation from the European countries for their part in the enslavement of Africans, and have kept the movement for redress alive within their communities in the United Kingdom, by giving lectures, doing workshops and making television appearances to argue the case for compensation from these European governments.

The Pan African Society Community Forum (PASCF), Alkebulan Revivalist Movement(ARM), the All-African People's Revolutionary Party (AAPRP) and Black History Studies UK have organised around education, identity, culture, business and political concerns. They have continued to develop and seek to maintain the links with the communities in the United Kingdom, the islands, the mainland and Africa. Caribbean Labour Solidarity's (CLS) first president and founder, Richard Hart, was born in Jamaica in 1917. He lived and worked in Jamaica, Grenada, Guyana and Britain. He recorded the history and struggles of the enslaved peoples in the Caribbean, as well as being one of the founder members of the trade union movement in the Caribbean. All these organisations and many, many more supported community issues first as small groups, then as larger associations as their community base grew.

The Windrush generation contributed significantly to music and sports in Britain, as many of the United Kingdom's sports teams were and are often made up of their children and grandchildren. There was no objection to them being in sports or music because white British society believed that they were only talented in these areas and that athletics, music and manual work was their natural place in British society. Island musicians had walked off the Windrush in 1948 singing calypso songs; these singers would be at the forefront of British music in subsequent years. Harold Adolphus Phillips from Trinidad (Lord Woodbine), an island musician and passenger on the Windrush, would later manage Britain's most famous pop group, the Beatles at the start of their career while promoting island music throughout Britain.

Alexander D Great - calypsonian, versatile musician, teacher, composer and broadcaster - came to Britain as a young child from Trinidad. His most significant contribution has been to keep the island's music alive in many institutions, schools, colleges, universities, carnival and on the BBC. He has fused calypso with other present-day musical styles and is known for kaiso, he continues to use calypso as social commentary in Britain. One of his many songs drew attention to the government's response to the murder of 13 black youths who burnt to death in a fire in New Cross in London in 1981. His song, '13 Dead and Nothing Said' underlines the struggle for justice faced by the Windrush generation and their children since 1948.

The Ex-servicemen from the islands and the mainland returning to the United Kingdom before and after the Windrush would also add to the legacy of black music in Britain. Their children born in the islands, the mainland or in Britain would make the kind of music that would change and influence British music forever. Allan Wilmot a World War II, veteran and his fellow islanders formed the Southlanders in 1950 and had a hit single in 1957, they also appeared on television in the pop show Six-Five Special and Crackerjack, children's programmes.

They were followed by such singers as Cy Grant, Billy Ocean, Eddie Grant and the Equals, The Real Thing, High Tension, Steel Pulse, Musical Youth, Errol Brown and Hot Chocolate, The Foundations, Aswad, Maxi Priest, Dizzee Rascal and Jazzie B. Musicians and songwriters such as Joan Armatrading and Courtney Pine gave the community a range of musical styles. Dennis Bovell and Janet

Kay gave their community and Britain 'lovers rock'. These musical traditions were born in Africa, perfected in the plantations of the islands and the American mainland and further developed in Britain.

Shirley Thompson, the musical composer, was born in London to island parents. She grew up and studied music at the London Borough of Newham's music school. Ms Thompson became the first woman in Europe to have composed and conducted a symphony within the past 40 years. She has written and performed several pieces for the BBC, Sadler's Wells and Carlton Television. Her musical compositions have been staged in many countries outside the United Kingdom. Some of her major works and artistic commissions have celebrated landmarks in African and the Diaspora's history.

In the early days, the sound men played the music the BBC and the radio stations would not play. They and the small record shops in the island communities throughout Britain were the primary source of music for the island communities in those years, and especially for the youth. They kept the island and the mainland music alive in the United Kingdom until the BBC had to play it because they had made the islander's music acceptable and fashionable. The sound men carried on the traditions established in the islands and in Britain by creating their own individual sound systems and clientele, especially at carnival time for years. They gave the youth an introduction to music that they may not have had in their mainstream schools. The steel pans found favour in many schools and institutions as a celebration of Caribbean culture and became a symbol of multi-cultural Britain. They were first played in Britain by Arthur Aldwyn Bosco Holder on the BBC in 1950. He was a painter and dance troop performer from Trinidad.

Pirate radio stations also played a significant role in the development of black music in the United Kingdom in the early days, although many of them are no longer broadcasting. The first black FM music radio station was transmitted from Neasden, London by Leroy Anderson in 1981. It was called the Dread Broadcasting Corporation. Genesis, Magic 105 and Colourful Radio stations still serve the community today. Choice FM was co-founded by Neil Kenlock, Patrick Berry and Yvonne Thompson. Neil Kenlock is a child of the Windrush generation; he came to Britain to join his parents in 1963. He is also associated with the founding of the lifestyle magazine, *Root*, along with Patrick Berry. In the early days, he worked for the *West Indian World* newspaper as a photographer and his well-published photograph 'Keep Britain White', documents attitudes to the migrant communities in Britain after 1948.

As a young boy, Charlie Phillip watched the tourist ships dock in Kingston Harbour, later he saw migrants leaving the island for England after 1948. In 1956, he also left the island and joined his parents in Notting Hill, London where they had a café. It was a run-down area of London, many people from the islands and the mainland lived there. Oswald Mosely and his fascist thugs operated in the area and tried to drive them out. Kelso Cochrane was murdered in Notting Hill in 1959. Charlie was an altar boy at the church where Kelso Cochrane's funeral service was held. He saw the Notting Hill riots and the community's protests at the killing.

Charlie taught himself photography and worked as a photographer taking pictures of film stars as well as his community in London. His book 'How Great Thou Art' (2014) records the funerals of the island and the mainland migrants in Britain. The book brings to the fore the tradition and importance of funerals in the islands and the mainland during and after slavery and for the community in Britain. The burial of Africans were important celebrations on the sugar plantations for the survivors. Death was their collective triumph over the slave masters, the guarantee of total freedom and the return of the ancestors to their families in Africa and a healthy afterlife.

The annual Notting Hill Carnival is said to have been founded by Claudia Jones, Sam King and other community members after the riots. Colin Prescod came to Britain as a young boy from Trinidad in 1958, to join his mother in Notting Hill. He has been resident there since then and has seen and documented the changes from an immigrant and white working-class neighbourhood, to one currently populated by the middle and wealthier classes. Colin is an academic and taught at a London University before becoming a filmmaker, commissioning editor for a broadcasting company and writer. He is the chair of the Institute of Race Relations and campaigned to get the

Docklands Museum located on the site where sugar and rum from the islands and the mainland were processed during and after slavery.

Notting Hill is still the home of the carnival 70 years after many of the Windrush generations made their first homes there. Carnival takes place at the end of August each year, it is the most prominent multiracial and multicultural event in the United Kingdom. The streets of Notting Hill have changed enormously, as well as being gentrified it is now the home of the very wealthy. These new arrivals would like to erase the islands and the mainland community's past presence in the area completely; by removing carnival from its streets at the end of August each year. Many of these wealthy residents, like many of the white middle classes that have moved into neighbourhoods that were formerly the homes of the Windrush generation and their children; do not want to be part of a tolerant multiracial, multicultural community and society, even for two days each year. However, the community is organising and campaigning to ensure that carnival remains there and is controlled by them and their representatives. Mr Prescod is a member of the campaign to keep carnival in Notting Hill.

The young people excelled in all areas of sports, they were encouraged by schools in the early years to take up this discipline rather than study academic subjects. The community had to pressure these institutions to offer their children a more comprehensive curriculum. Linford Christie, Colin Jackson, Tessa Sanderson, Daley Thompson, Dwaine Chambers, John Regis, Denise Lewis, Kelly Holmes and the newcomers Asher Phillips, Desiree Henry, Dina Asher-Smith, Daryll Neita, Dwayne Cowan and Matthew Hudson-Smith stood out in track-and-field events. In boxing, the greats are Lennox Lewis, Frank Bruno, Nigel Benn, Chris Eubank, Michael Watson and Nicola Adams.

The children and grandchildren of the Windrush's generation dominated football too, as soon as the opportunities were available to them. In the beginning, black football players were often left out of international teams because it was felt that Britain's football teams should be white. Bananas were thrown at them on the pitch, and they were abused at away games in the United Kingdom and Europe by white football supporters. Herman Ouseley founded the campaign to kick 'racism' out of sports because of the open displays of racism at football matches in Britain and abroad. He was supported by Cyrille Regis and other black players who experienced racist chanting while playing. However, English football managers were always acquitted when allegations of racism were made against them by Black male and female players. It is noticeable that other professions in Britain did not set up campaigns to kick racism out of their occupations.

Cyrille Regis was born in French Guiana in 1958 and came to England in 1963 with his parents. *The Independent* newspaper, in its tribute to him in January 2018, stated: "He was a trailblazer for black football players in the early years, at a time of high racial tension. He endured appalling abuse from supporters in Britain and Europe but overcame racism, bigotry and threats and was the inspiration for the black players who came after him. He played his part in England becoming a more tolerant society." Nice one Cyrille.

Cyrille's contemporaries and those he inspired to take up the game performed brilliantly at the club and international level. They are Clyde Best, Luther Blissett, Garth Crooks, Ian Wright, Dwight Yorke, Paul Ince, Jermain Defoe, Viv Anderson, Dion Dublin, Sol Campbell, Laurie Cunningham, Brendon Batson, Rio and Les Ferdinand, David James, Jermaine Jenas, Aron Lennon and many, many more players.

Ellery Hanley was a player and later coach of Great Britain's rugby league teams; Desmond Douglas was eleven times English table tennis champion.

The building trades provided a lifeline in the early years for the Windrush generation and their children, if they were not recruited to work in the Post Office, The NHS, British Rail or London Transport. Many of these workers had building and engineering skills before they came to the United Kingdom, many had served lengthy apprenticeships in the islands and the mainland after leaving school. The men worked as carpenters, plasterers, builders, plumbers, electricians, and painters. These skilled crafts allowed some of them to set up their own business which supported their children who later went into the professions. Many made good money in the booming years of the building trade and built up property portfolios, they had to tighten their belts in the downturns in the industry.

Silbert Frazer came to England from rural Jamaica in 1961, as a young man, where he had completed an apprenticeship in plumbing. He set up a small business with a friend Granville Lewis who had migrated earlier. Silbert is now retired but spent fifty-five years working as a plumber. In the 1980s, the daughters of the Windrush generation took the opportunity to be trained in the building arts, Cynthia Pottinger retrained and worked as a carpenter until her retirement.

The skills of the building trades are vital for every society, they have positively served the Windrush generation and their children in the United Kingdom. As a community, we believe that these skills stand alongside every other profession that society considers desirable and well paid. The community value these skills highly and we should encourage our young men and women to get these skills if they want to. However, Steve McQueen has rightly pointed out that he will not accept, that he and his community and school students are only suitable for the jobs British society, believe they should do. His school, further, higher education and career personifies the potential and abilities of all peoples and especially the islands and the mainland communities' children in the United Kingdom.

The Empire Windrush also brought the island's children and their children, who would become future mayors, judges, lawyers, barristers, MP's, Peers of the Realm, TV personalities, actors, hair salon proprietors, famous restaurateurs and chefs as a matter of course.

Rustie Lee came to the United Kingdom as a child. She studied at a local college after leaving school and became a master baker and chef. She set up the first Caribbean Silver Service Restaurant in Handsworth Birmingham, later she became and is still a TV chef and personality. The Atlantic Bakery in Brixton market and the mixed Blessing Bakery in Walworth Road provided generations of islanders and mainlanders with patties, bun, bread and other delicacies, over the decades and still does so today. Ainsley Harriot, also cooked on British and American television and talked continuously about his Jamaican mother's influence on his cooking style.

Sam King, a World War II veteran, community activists and passenger on the Windrush, became Mayor of Southwark in London in 1983. Bernie Grant, Diane Abbott and David Lammy have served the island community and their constituents over the years as Members of Parliament.

Diane Abbott organised and promoted the yearly 'Black Child' conference bringing together parents and the community to discuss, campaign and find solutions to the schooling of the community's children. She also sponsored the yearly award ceremonies, to acknowledge the educational achievements of those pupils who were succeeding in the school system. This helped to challenge the stereotype that all the community's children were failing, as well as encouraging and raising the confidence of other students to realise their full potential. She was the first black woman to have a seat in the House of Commons.

David Lammy has campaigned against inequalities in the justice system's sentencing of Black and Minority Ethnic prisoners, who are more likely to get longer sentences than white offenders for the same misdemeanours.

The late Bernie Grant came to Britain in 1963, studied engineering and became a trade union official and then a ward councillor in Tottenham, London, where many islanders and mainlanders settled. He was elected a Member of Parliament in 1987 and supported the struggles of black youth in his constituency and the United Kingdom. The Bernie Grant Centre in Tottenham, London honours his contribution to his community and British society.

Doreen Lawrence came to England as a very young child in the early 1960s and was educated in Britain. She is the mother of Stephen Lawrence who was murdered by racists in 1993. She and Stephen's father, Neville Lawrence, campaigned tirelessly to get justice for their son when the police failed to investigate adequately and bring to court those who murdered their son. Doreen and Neville Lawrence's persistent pursuit of justice for their son resulted in the eventual arrest and conviction of two men for his murder. It also led to the MacPherson Report (1999) which acknowledged that the Metropolitan Police force was and is 'institutionally racist' because of its investigation of their son's murder. Their unceasing pursuit of justice is an excellent achievement for the Windrush generation and their children because they held the police force and British society to account, for the racist practices in its institutions and forced British society to acknowledge racism. Doreen Lawrence was awarded the order of the British Empire in 2003 and is now Baroness Lawrence of Clarendon.

Valerie Amos - Baroness Amos - came to Britain from Guyana. She is an academic and was made a Labour peer in 1997. Ms Amos served as a politician and Diplomat. She was secretary of State for International development and British High Commissioner to Australia. She is now the Director of the School for African and Oriental Studies and is the first black woman in Britain to hold this post.

The Reverend Sybil Phoenix came to Britain from Guyana in 1965. From the beginning she has been active in her community. She worked tirelessly to improve the life chances of young people especially young women. She fostered over 100 girls within the borough in which she lived. Later she set up a hostel for homeless young women. She was also instrumental in setting up the first purpose-built black youth club after the New Cross Fire in 1981. Mrs Phoenix has served the community in various capacities for 60 years. She was the first black woman to be awarded an MBE in the United Kingdom for her community service.

In the 1960s, Len Dyke set up one of the first black businesses in London soon after arriving from Jamaica in 1955. Initially, he sold records from the islands, later he began to make and sell hair and beauty products to his fellow islanders. The business was expanded when Dudley Dryden joined. They laid the foundations for black enterprise culture at a period in history when the received wisdom was that black people could not do big business. They began by selling their products out of boxes, but as the company grew they set up their first shop, on West Green Road, in Tottenham, North London. It evolved into a multi-million-pound enterprise, and they became Britain's first black multi-millionaires. They set up the annual Afro Hair and Beauty Expo.

Winston Isaacs opened the first Caribbean hair salon in the West End of London, called 'Splinters' in 1970. It trained many African-Caribbean hair stylists and they later styled the hair of many of the rising stars of the islands' community. Splinters also began a trend in which many African-Caribbean people set up hairdressing establishments outside their homes. Lloyd's Barbers in Peckham, South London, became the set for 'Desmonds', a popular television comedy.

The Windrush generation and their children have shown, without a doubt that they are the worthy descendants of the enslaved Africans who liberated themselves in 1838. They have fearlessly taken on the struggles the enslaved Africans began for the improvement of all the African community, wherever they might be. They have stamped their African heritage firmly within the metropolis, from 1948, and have continually challenged the structural and deep-rooted inequalities that were and are significant features of British and world society.

Oh, I nearly forgot to include the most valuable compliment and achievement, that Africa's Diaspora has given to their motherland Africa and their illustrious ancestors who abolished slavery. They took me (Anancy, Anansi, Ananse), with them in the belly of the galleons to the islands and the mainland of the Americas, while they laboured in the cane pieces in their pain and grief. They did not leave me behind in the Americas after their liberation. Gladly, they took me to the next stage of their journey to the United Kingdom and Europe, again to inspire and comfort them in their daily struggles, to improve the quality of their lives and build constructive images of the African race. This is the strength of all races and cultures.

The future social and economic well-being of Africa and its Diaspora are perilous in whichever part of the world they reside. To improve and guaranteed a viable future, for all peoples of African descent and humanity, we must work together as equal human beings, women and men. The process of African liberation and human emancipation is not a competition or a replica of European hierarchical structures and conduct which excludes those who have already been disempowered, by the discriminatory social and economic organisation of white British and world society.

Black and African best describes Africa's Diaspora. These are not states of mind or physical being that can be conferred on, or be taken away by individuals or groups because this perpetuates the discriminatory practices and behaviour of European society experienced by the island and the mainland communities and their ancestors from their enslavement.

African culture personifies humanity, hospitality, humility, tolerance, respect for community members, but especially for the elderly, and a recognition and celebration of everyone as viable and competent human beings with a variety of skills, knowledge and experiences to enhance the motherland, her diaspora, the world community and humankind. Each and every one of us is and must be part of the solution to our total political, economic, social, cultural and personal liberation. The Windrush scandal, 70 years after the docking of the ship underlines the struggle the Windrush generation continue to face in the mother country. It reinforces the need for the community to work together, women and men young and old to challenge the structural inequalities and racism in British society.

Reparation March 1st August 2017, Brixton
Photo: B. Ellis

Sign indicating Windrush Square Brixton.
Photo: B. Ellis

Carnival procession 2017-Notting Hill Photo: B. Ellis

Len Garrison's ACER (Afro-Caribbean Education Resource) teaching and learning resources were first housed in a primary school in Vauxhall, London as a resource for the Black community, teachers, pupils and the wider community. This resource laid the foundations for the Black Cultural Archives when the Inner London Education Authority was broken up into Local Education Authorities. Len co-founded the Black Cultural Archives now housed in Windrush Square.

Photo: B. Ellis

African Remembrance Day 2017 at the Docklands Museum, London
Photo: B. Ellis

Windrush Square Brixton
Photo: B. Ellis